C000131937

Also available f   Kogan Page

BE YOUR OWN
ACCOUNTANT

BE YOUR OWN
ACCOUNTANT

PHILIP McNEILL AND
SARAH J P HOWARTH

KOGAN
PAGE

While every care has been taken in the preparation of this book, the authors and publishers can accept no responsibility for loss occasioned to any person acting or refraining from action as a result of any statement in it.

First published in 1994

Kogan Page Limited
120 Pentonville Road
London N1 9JN

© Sarah JP Howarth and Philip McNeill

British Library Cataloguing in Publication Data

A CIP record for this book is available from the British Library.

ISBN 0-7494-1230-5

Typeset by Books Unlimited (Nottm), Sutton-in-Ashfield NG17 1AL

Printed and bound in Great Britain by Clays Ltd, St Ives plc

Contents

Preface

Asking an accountant questions costs money, so be your own accountant.

The questions that crop up most frequently in a professional office concern income tax, National Insurance and VAT. If you want to know how to set about answering such questions for yourself, this book will set you on the right track.

'Here be dragons' it used to say on old maps. But there were no dragons – only unfamiliar places. The same is true in business. The Inland Revenue, the DSS, Customs and Excise may seem like dragons. But if you know how to deal with them, the dragons disappear.

This book will show you how to deal with the authorities, what they expect of you, and how to act on your own behalf. It takes you through the issues involved in keeping records, preparing and understanding accounts, finding out what expenses you can set against tax, filling in a tax return, and checking a tax bill.

Other questions that set an accountant's phone ringing include business planning and financial management. Unfortunately, there are simply not enough pages here to deal comprehensively with these topics as well. Other books in this series, such as *Cash Flow and How to Improve It* by Leon Hopkins fill the gap.

1. Where to get advice

Getting it right first time

Imagine that you are your own accountant – you're paying yourself for finding things out. Perhaps you are paying yourself a pound a minute, or more – such things do happen. In this case you will want to find out as much as you can in the shortest time possible in order to avoid a large bill.

The key to doing this is to plan your time, and to plan your time you need to organise your questions logically. You need to know what to ask, and whom to ask it of. If you were on the staff of a large firm of chartered accountants, there would be any number of experts you could call on for help. You might direct your query to any one of a number of different departments – the personal tax department, investments, corporate tax, audit, or small trader department, for example.

As a taxpayer or a business person with a question to ask, you too have options and sources of help.

Where to go for advice

Some people or organisations deal with only one specific type of problem; others will deal with many. On the other hand, perhaps you don't want to see a person at all – perhaps you would prefer to research the problem using libraries and printed material. When you are choosing where to go for advice, it is useful to have a clear idea of what you are looking for. The following may influence your decision:

• Cost

- Solution or information?
- One-off or continuing advice?
- Interview, telephone or print?
- Location
- Mobility
- Meeting face to face
- Confidentiality
- One appointment or many?
- Feeling at ease
- Accuracy
- Appropriateness
- Choosing who you meet
- Specialists

Cost

Are you prepared to pay for advice? Even some bodies like the Rural Development Commission charge for certain specialist advice.

You may have a specific budget in mind when you look for advice. You need to know what the advice is going to cost you. There is little point in spending £50 on advice when you are chasing a tax refund of £45.

Solution or information?

Do you want to explain your circumstances to someone else, so that they can give you an overall solution, or are you mainly looking for information in order to make your own decision?

One-off or continuing advice?

Is the advice or information you seek one-off, or part of an on-going relationship?

Interview, telephone or print?

Do you want to be able to discuss your problems face to face, or are you content with telephone contact, or with printed or written information?

Location

Can you travel, or would you prefer someone to call on you?

Mobility

Is it difficult for you to get out of the house or office during normal business hours? Do you have problems with transport and need a local service?

Meeting face to face

Some people find it easier to explain themselves and get a good grip on the problem by meeting face to face. You may prefer to meet someone at your home, informally, or a more formal office environment may suit you.

Confidentiality

How important to you is it that your affairs remain absolutely private? Do you want to discuss your business with someone whom you know, even by sight?

One appointment or many?

You might not want to have to explain your problem to a series of people. Would you prefer to deal with someone who can answer all your queries and put your mind at rest in one go?

Feeling at ease

You want to feel at ease when asking for advice – free to discuss what matters to you without feeling overawed or pressurised into agreeing to any particular course of action or timescale.

Accuracy

You want to know that the advice you get is accurate and up to date.

Appropriateness

You want to be sure that your adviser fully understands your circumstances.

Choosing who you meet

For a wide variety of reasons, you may have specific ideas about who you want to talk to. You may need to talk to someone who is fluent in a particular language; you may prefer to talk to someone of a particular age, race, sex or religion.

Specialists

Your problems may be quite out of the ordinary. You may then need a specialist to deal with them. If you are dealing with a complex problem or questions that are interrelated, it is probably best to talk to someone.

When you have considered these factors, you should have a good idea of the best approach for you. The next sections will give you a more detailed idea of what to expect from each information source.

Useful publications

There are some publications that it may be worth purchasing, and others you may be able to find in libraries.

Tax publications

The most simple and useful publication you can buy is a set of tax tables. These are produced by a number of publishers. They provide in one, small, inexpensive – under £3 in 1993 – booklet of about 60 pages, details of the available tax allowances, tax bands, rates and thresholds for the major taxes from National Insurance to stamp duty, and from VAT to capital gains tax. They usually give details for the current tax year, and the previous six years. They often also list the free leaflets produced by the tax authorities and provide an address from which these can be obtained. Armed with a set of tax tables, you should be able to start getting to grips with your tax problems.

The remainder of tax publications fall essentially into two groups. First, there are compilations of legislation which are usually annotated. Second, there is interpretative material, either on one specific topic or on a tax or group of taxes. In the latter group fall the many books of tax hints. The great advantage of such books is that they sift the legislation, and highlight specific matters for your attention. The great disadvantage is that they may take little account of your specific circumstances. It is also true that, as legislation changes rapidly, it is necessary to check that what you read is up to date.

Other publications

Libraries may also hold registers of grant-making bodies, books on personal finance and investment guides, law, and a range of publications on business-related matters. As with tax publications, caution is needed here. Check that the records are updated. A review of up-to-date periodicals and magazines, coupled with a look at relevant comprehensive books, should be time well spent.

Often the material you need to consult in libraries will be for reference use only. If you can't get a book out, or need something to review at home, a leaflet may be the answer.

Leaflets and press releases

There are hundreds of leaflets, produced by various bodies, which can help you to be your own accountant. Most are only a phone call away. You can obtain a list of publications free by post from your local Benefits or Contributions Agency, VAT Office, Inland Revenue Enquiry Office or Companies House. Up-to-date guidance on new or controversial areas can be obtained in the form of press releases from the press office of the relevant government department.

Tax leaflets

Of the wide number of tax-related publications, perhaps the most useful are likely to be the Inland Revenue's *List of Extra Statutory Concessions*, and the Customs and Excise *VAT Guide*. The *List of Extra Statutory Concessions* details numerous relaxations of the laws, and is designed to correct perceived anomalies in the drafted legislation, or to facilitate the administration of the law. The *VAT Guide* sets out the basic application of VAT and indicates other leaflets which may be helpful.

The Inland Revenue will also supply at a low cost Business Economic Notes for a range of industries. These provide an introduction to the main economic factors involved in each particular industry, and a guide to how such businesses operate.

Leaflets of use in various situations are listed below, with reference numbers. Reference 'IR' indicates Inland Revenue leaflets, NP, NI and FB are Benefits Agency leaflets.

For employees
- Pay As You Earn   IR 34
- Income tax and the unemployed   IR 41
- National Insurance for employees   NP 28

For married couples
- Income tax and married couples   IR 80
- Separation, divorce and maintenance payments   IR 39

For people with savings
- A guide for people with savings   IR 110
- TESSA tax-free interest for taxpayers   IR 114
- Are you paying too much tax on your savings?   IR 127

For people in business
- Starting in business   IR 28
- Simple tax accounts   IR 104
- Thinking of working for yourself?   IR 57
- How your profits are taxed   IR 105
- Capital allowances for vehicles and machinery   IR 106
- National Insurance contributions for self-employed people (Class 2 and Class 4)   NP 18
- Self-employed?   FB 30

For people in the construction industry
- Construction industry tax deduction scheme   IR 14/15
- Construction industry: conditions for getting a sub-contractor's tax certificate   IR 40

For employers
- Thinking of taking someone on?   IR 53
- Employer's further guide to Pay As You Earn   P7
- National Insurance manual for employers   NI 269

Other leaflets

Leaflets are also produced by many other bodies, from the Rural Development Commission to the clearing banks. Those produced by the Rural Development Commission, for example, include details of grant assistance available in specific areas, while those produced by the clearing banks often provide valuable information for those starting in business.

In summary, if you have a specific query on a single topic, leaflets may well provide your answer in the most cost-effective manner possible. If you have numerous queries, you may still find leaflets valuable, but it may be best to talk to someone before you act.

Someone to talk to

There are a number of people who will listen and give advice. They include:

- The Citizens' Advice Bureau
- The Inland Revenue
- The Department of Social Security
- Customs and Excise
- Government agencies
- Companies House
- Professional firms

The Citizens' Advice Bureau

The CAB aims to provide a free, independent and confidential service, advising individuals irrespective of age, gender, race, religion or any other circumstance. A wide range of information is held on social, financial, legal and other issues, from eligibility for social security benefits to debt counselling and how to complain about noisy neighbours. The CAB maintains a relatively small number of paid staff, supported by a large number of volunteer workers. All volunteers are required to attend a training course before starting work. Some specialist workers may also attend bureau sessions, although this service is most likely to be found in large urban centres. Such workers range from lawyers to debt counsellors to accountants.

The strength of the organisation is its central information system which distributes standard information files to all bureaux with regular updates. All workers are trained in the use of the information system, and thus have access to an increasingly wide-ranging data base.

Whatever your query, you can expect to meet someone who can look up information for you. Workers are able to provide: information on specific queries; help in completing forms; guidance as to how tax codes or state benefits are calculated; advice on training schemes or financial assistance available for start-up businesses; local information specific to your area; and advice on many other issues. They may be able to contact and deal with other organisations on your behalf and, when necessary, point you in the right direction if a query becomes too complex. Enquiries may be made by phone, or in person.

The Inland Revenue

Although many taxpayers tend to look on the relationship with the Revenue as somewhat gladiatorial, the Revenue will provide a certain level of assistance with your tax affairs. Used correctly, the Revenue is another source of free information. Before you enter the lions' den, it is worth having a clear picture of exactly what the Revenue can do for you. To assess whether the Revenue can help in your circumstances, the question to bear in mind is: what help is the Revenue there to give? And, just as important, what does it *not* set out to do?

There are certain basic parameters within which the taxpayer's relationship with the Revenue is supposed to operate, and there are certain rights which the taxpayer may expect to be accorded. These are set out in *The Tax Payer's Charter*. A copy of this document is attached to a variety of Revenue forms, such as 11[1993] 'Filling in Your Tax Return'. The Charter explains the service you 'are entitled to expect' of the Revenue. As an outline guide, defining how far the Revenue will help you to be your own accountant, key points are shown here.

The Revenue must be fair:

- By settling your tax affairs impartially
- By expecting you to pay only what is due under the law
- By treating everyone with equal fairness

It will help you:
- To get your tax affairs right
- To understand your rights and obligations
  - By providing clear leaflets and forms
  - By giving you information and assistance at their enquiry offices
  - By being courteous at all times

This then is the Revenue on what the Revenue can do. Local Revenue staff will provide factual answers to factual questions, or give advice based on their understanding of your circumstances. The Revenue should be able to explain, for example, how your PAYE code is calculated, or whether you are entitled to a refund of tax on investment income, or what business expenses you are allowed to deduct from your income before tax. Their role is restricted to income tax and corporation tax, although on some occasions they will also deal with capital taxes, such as inheritance tax and capital gains tax.

Revenue role
- Specific answers to specific questions
- Income tax and corporation tax
- Capital taxes

How far will this help you? To answer this, let's look at what the Revenue is not there to do. It is not there to help you arrange your affairs in order to minimise your tax liability. To look again at *The Tax Payer's Charter*: the brief is 'to get your tax affairs right'. Right? Accurate – yes. But arranged in the way most beneficial to you? Possibly so, but not necessarily. 'Expecting you to pay only what is due under the law' – whose interpretation of the law? The Revenue is not designed to help you plan your tax affairs for the future, nor to highlight all the possible consequences of any particular course of action. It cannot give a comprehensive picture of your tax affairs, in that VAT and, to a degree, capital taxes will be left out of the equation. And to a certain extent, it is operating in a vacuum. Staff may not have immediate access to all information if, for example, your affairs are dealt with by more than one tax office. The answer they give is likely to be on the basis of information supplied; there may be matters which you do not disclose, not believing them to be of importance, which would materially affect calculations. Whereas a trained professional adviser should automatically build up a comprehensive picture of your circumstances, the Revenue does not aim to give a bespoke service of this kind.

Much depends on who you speak to. You may speak to someone at a fairly junior level on the telephone. You can ask for an Inspector, in other words someone at a senior level of competence. But he or she will not be briefed on your circumstances beforehand. Remember: the Revenue can, and does, make mistakes. These can prove expensive if you have based decisions on them.

Outside Revenue brief
- Minimising tax liability
- Interaction of taxes
- VAT
- Tax planning
- Scenarios arising from different courses of action
- Comprehensive picture of your affairs

Getting in touch

The mechanics of getting in touch are straightforward. Most local Revenue offices are generally open each weekday, from 8.30am to 4.30pm. You can make enquiries in person, by phone or by letter. Which tax office to approach is up to you. If you want a degree of anonymity, you can make a generalised enquiry of any office. Staff will try to help. But clearly the more you can describe your personal circumstances, the better placed Revenue staff will be to give an answer. For this reason your own tax office is an obvious port of call.

To get things running smoothly, it will help to be able to quote your tax reference number. Self-employed people can find this on tax bills and tax returns; employees on forms such as P45s and P60s issued by your employer.

The Department of Social Security

The Department of Social Security has recently been split into a number of different agencies. With the exception of Class 4, which is collected by the Inland Revenue, the Contributions Agency deals with National Insurance contributions. The Benefits Agency deals with any payments made to you – pensions and benefits. Written and telephone enquiries can be made, and opening hours are to be found in the local telephone directory. Many offices are open from 9.30am to 3.30pm. It always helps to have your National Insurance number to hand when contacting the DSS. The DSS in Newcastle can to help trace numbers which have been lost, although this is best done by post.

The Contributions Agency has a freephone line which offers advice to employers. The Benefits Agency operates a number of freephone numbers. These include lines in Chinese, Punjabi and Urdu, and a general freephone line supplying information on its services. These freephone numbers do not connect with your local office, which gives confidentiality, should you want a degree of anonymity in making a preliminary enquiry. As with the Inland Revenue, the role of these agencies is essentially factual, rather than planning or advisory.

Customs and Excise

Questions about VAT are different. They are the province of Customs and Excise. The day-to-day nature of the impact of VAT – and the VAT penalty regime – mean that VAT enquiries are treated in a formal manner.

Since the recent reorganisation, there are few truly 'local' VAT enquiry offices. Meeting a VAT officer face to face is thus fast becoming an unusual occurrence. It is most likely to happen only at a routine VAT compliance inspection visit (see below). All other contact with Customs and Excise is most likely to be written or by telephone.

Contacting Customs and Excise

VAT office procedure requires that you produce all your personal details before staff will address a query: your VAT registration number, the nature of your business, your name, business address, and so forth. Hypothetical questions – or anonymous ones – are virtually impossible. Certainly on any contentious issue, you would want an answer in writing. VAT is a practical tax, and Customs and Excise are essentially there to give practical advice. They cannot help with tax planning. The 'VAT Enquiries Guide', reference number 700.51.93, sets out the way that Customs and Excise operate when dealing with an enquiry.

Treading with care

Given that Customs and Excise have powers to impose sweeping penalties (see below), the golden rule is: if it's VAT, tread carefully. Do as much homework as possible before you contact Customs and Excise. Read the relevant leaflets which are all listed in 'VAT Publications' (700.13A.93). If you are a trader registered for VAT, read the VAT 'Notes' which come with your VAT return during the year, and keep up-to-date with recent or forthcoming changes to the legislation.

It pays to be well prepared in any dealings with Customs and Excise. If you make a mistake, voluntary disclosures do not usually attract the same penalties as errors discovered by Excise officers, for example, on a compliance visit. So don't put your head in the noose through ignorance of the law. Keeping abreast of VAT legislation and procedure is vital if you are to be your own accountant. Then if you do need to approach Customs and Excise on a difficult point, you are more likely to ask the right questions at the right time, and less likely to fall into unnecessary – and expensive – errors.

Government Agencies

The enterprise culture of the 1980s and 1990s has seen the expansion of numerous bodies which can provide help to the small business person. These include:

* Rural Development Commission
* Training and Enterprise Councils (TECs) in England and Wales and Local Enterprise Companies in Scotland (LECs)
* Local enterprise agencies

- Department of Trade and Industry regional offices

Rural Development Commission

The Commission helps to promote the economy of rural areas. Its target client base is given as English villages and towns with a population of under 10,000. Manufacturing and service industries with less than 20 full-time employees may be eligible for assistance from the Commission. There are certain specific types of business which are excluded from the Commission's remit, and details of these can be obtained from the Commission. Information packs can be sent out from the Commission's head office at 141 Castle Street, Salisbury, Wiltshire SP1 3TP, or by contacting your local office. (Details in the telephone directory.)

The types of service offered include:

- Meeting with a business adviser from the RDC
  Initial meeting free of charge. After this stage, recommendations for action can be made, with an estimate of fees for future involvement
- Meeting with RDC management accountants
  Help with extracting management information from your records, making presentations to potential lenders
- Advice on eligibility for loans and grants, some made specifically by the RDC, such as redundant building grants
- Technical training courses, such as forgework and farriery
- Advice on quality assurance
- Marketing advice
- Publications
- Business premises – workshops, etc, available in some locations

Training and Enterprise Councils

TECs, based in the local community, can assist unemployed people who want to start a business of their own. Job Centres can provide details of the assistance available. The CAB may also be able to provide information.

Local enterprise agencies

These can be run to ground through the local phone book, or by enquiring at the CAB. Some enterprise agencies can make loans or grants; all should be able to give advice on raising finance. Alternative bodies known as Business Links are being phased in here and 23 should be operative before the end of 1994.

Department of Trade and Industry regional offices

These regional offices can provide a range of services such as consultancy services in the fields of design, business planning, etc. Special help is available for areas designated as 'Assisted Areas'.

Companies House

If your query is about a limited company, it may be a good idea to try Companies House.

The role of Companies House is to act as a repository of information about companies. Many limited companies have to supply details to the Registrar of Companies there: all UK-registered, and some foreign-registered companies with places of business in the United Kingdom have to make a wide variety of returns to Companies House. This information is available to the public.

The services provided by Companies House include information about how, in general, companies are required by law to be run; and sophisticated search facilities enabling members of the public to obtain information about individual companies and their personnel. Companies House also has a general role in company formation and supervision.

General information

Companies House publishes a range of useful leaflets which set out many of the legal requirements affecting the running of a limited company. They are available by post, free of charge, from the Stationery Section at Companies House, Crown Way, Cardiff CF4 3UZ. Subjects dealt with include directors' responsibilities, limited partnerships, accounting reference dates, liquidation and insolvency, new companies, company names, duties of company secretaries, business names and business ownership, requirements to disclose information and penalties which may be imposed for infringement of company law, and the format in which documents may be presented to Companies House. They are easy to read, and explain the tortuous workings of company law in a succinct form.

Specific information

The other main area where Companies House can provide information is from its comprehensive data base. If you have questions about a specific company – or the people who run it – this is the service for you.

To use the service, you will need to know the name of the company, or the name of the person (for instance, a company director) you wish to investigate. It may also be useful to have the registered number of the company. This should be shown on all the company invoices and business stationery. These basic facts give you an open sesame to a range of details:

- Names and addresses of directors
- Name and address of company secretary
- Their previous appointments
- Details of any disqualifications
- Details of the company's registered office
- Documents, such as accounts and returns, filed by the company

Data of this kind may prove useful in a variety of situations. If, for example, you are about to do business with a limited company and would like to find out how healthy its finances are before you act, the ability to look at accounts (some smaller companies do not have to file their profit and loss account and other details) can help you to make up your mind about how much credit it is reasonable to extend. It can also be a useful tool if you are thinking of setting up a business in a new area and would like to know something about your potential competitors.

Companies House is a gold-mine of information but it is available only at a cost; information about search fees can be obtained from Companies House. Searches can be done in person, by post, through a search agency or, most recently, for a subscriber fee, on line at your office using the Companies House Direct Service.

Professional Firms

Professional services may occasionally be of use even if you are thinking of being your own accountant.

Accountants

Most professional firms will be able to advise you on all the points described above on a continuing basis. But they may also be prepared to give one-off advice on specific areas. How do you choose who to go to? Accountants come in all shapes and sizes – with letters after their name and without. Clearly the more highly qualified, the more comprehensive the service on offer. The following list sets out the main organisations to which qualified accountants belong, and the designatory initials which are used:

- Institute of Chartered Accountants in Scotland – CA
- Institute of Chartered Accountants in England and Wales – ACA and FCA
- Chartered Institute of Certified Accountants – ACCA and FCCA
- Institute of Taxation (for specialist tax advice) – ATII and FTII

Basis of fees

Having chosen your adviser, the next item on your agenda may well be finding out how much you are likely to be charged. Many firms will provide an initial interview without charge, and some may provide fixed or scale fees for particular work, such as income tax repayment claims. But, by and large, the cost will depend on the amount of time spent dealing with your affairs.

Minimising fees

There may be ways in which you can keep fees to a minimum. The simplest points can often pay dividends. Formulate your questions as succinctly as possible. Read any letters you receive carefully. If you are asked to provide information, deliver it all in one go. It is always more time-consuming and expensive if your adviser has to keep stopping and starting a job. If asked to sign and return forms, don't let too much time slip by. Reminder letters cost money. If you have written out details for inspection, are your figures legible? Will the individual behind the desk have to add up your figures three times – and add to your bill three-fold – to see if it's a 3 or a 5, a 2 or a 4 that you have written? Just as fundamentally, is your handwriting legible? It may be perfectly obvious to you that GRM*P!FZ inscribed on your cheque stub in fact reads 'Franklin, tallow chandler and printer' but it may take a lot longer for your adviser to cotton on. And minimising time is the most certain way to minimise the fees you have to pay.

Using the charging structure

There are other ways of minimising fees and maximising the benefit you get from the money you spend. You should always be aware of the seniority of the person you are dealing with. In general, the more senior, the higher the charging rate. Use the charging structure to your advantage. Don't insist on speaking to the senior partner if all you want to do is find out if your business records have been finished with. When you telephone, give the receptionist enough information to be able to put your question straight through to the right member of staff. Don't entertain senior partners to your views on the iniquities of the Inland Revenue. They may well agree, but they can't change the system, and in the mean time time ticks by. Common sense can help you to get the most from your relationship with a professional firm.

2. Dealing with the Inland Revenue

If you are going to be your own accountant, you need to be able to deal with the Inland Revenue. It helps to have a clear understanding of the work of the Revenue as well as basic Revenue administrative procedures, and your rights of appeal. You also need to know who you need to speak to at the Revenue, and which department you will find them in.

The structure of the Revenue

The Inland Revenue oversees and enforces the laws relating to the assessment and payment of taxes. The basic administrative procedures are set out in law in the Taxes Management Act 1970. To save you a diet of somewhat indigestible legislation, the sections below give a guide on how to deal with the Inland Revenue and what to expect from it.

The agreeing of tax liabilities and the collection of money due are dealt with by two separate sections of the Revenue. Liabilities are agreed with the Inspector of Taxes. Payment is made to and enforced by the Collector of Taxes.

Organisational change is currently being implemented whereby local tax and collection offices will be transformed into TSOs (taxpayer service offices), supported by TDOs (tax district offices) and TAOs (taxpayer assistance offices). At present, few of these new-style offices exist, and the exercise is likely to take up to ten years to implement fully.

HM Inspectors of Taxes

Most of the forms you receive from the Revenue come from your District Inspector of Taxes. His or her name appears on tax returns and assessments, and on printed Revenue stationery. The District Inspector is responsible for the administration of taxes in a particular district, often your local geographical area. The actual work of agreeing tax liabilities is delegated to a number of Assistant Inspectors, who are supported by a number of other Revenue officers.

HM Collectors of Taxes

Usually the collection of tax is relatively straightforward. The majority of payments are processed centrally by the Inland Revenue. The process starts to become more complex where, for example, a taxpayer delays making payment. Here the case may be referred to a local Collector of Taxes for further action. The job of Collectors and their staff is to obtain money owing and payable to the Revenue. They are not concerned with whether the amounts are the final liability; it may be that the assessment is to be revised in the near future – the Collector will collect the tax shown as due just the same. Collectors also collect money due on estimated assessments.

Time is of the essence in dealing with the Collector. It is important to reply to all letters promptly. If you are not paying the tax demanded for a technical reason, you should set out your reasons in full. In cases of financial difficulty, the Collector will often agree to payment of tax by instalments. If you are experiencing a cash-flow problem, and feel that an instalment arrangement would help, it is always best to contact the Collector as soon as possible to set things in motion. Acting before you begin to get red reminders makes for plainer sailing.

If a taxpayer fails to agree a position with the Collector, action in the county court follows. In such proceedings, the Collector of Taxes acts as plaintiff and the taxpayer as defendant. In the final analysis, if judgment is given against the taxpayer, all the usual enforcement procedures may be brought into play. These include the use of bailiffs.

Appeals procedures: the Commissioners of the Inland Revenue

In most cases it should be possible to reach agreement with your Inspector of Taxes. If this fails, the next step is to refer the case to the Commissioners of the Inland Revenue. They can be involved on the request of either the taxpayer or the Inspector.

The Commissioners are an independent body, rather like JPs. Their remit is to arbitrate in cases of dispute between the taxpayer and the Revenue. There are two groups of Commissioners: the Special Commissioners and the General Commissioners. Special Commissioners have a degree of expert tax knowledge. Usually only contentious technical questions are referred to them.

General Commissioners have wide-ranging powers to bring about agreement between the taxpayer and the Revenue. Their decisions on questions of fact are usually binding. Appeal may be made against their decisions but only on points of law. Again, it is open to either the taxpayer or the Revenue to take the case on to the next level. But to do so the dissenting party must make his or her position clear as soon as the Commissioners' decision is given.

Appeal from the General Commissioners is to the High Court, and eventually to the House of Lords. This is the sequence of events that can lead to your name being immortalised in the title of a new tax precedent. It is also likely to be extremely time-consuming and, by this stage, expensive. Going this far demands that you are more than ordinarily convinced about your case.

Who deals with what?

When income tax was introduced, it was thought a disgraceful invasion of privacy for any Revenue official to have a picture of the *whole* of a taxpayer's income. To make the tax more palatable, it was therefore decided to set up separate offices to deal with the many different types of income then received by taxpayers. Taxpayers would make separate returns to each office: rental income statements would go to one office, statements of foreign income to another, UK dividends to a third, income from woodlands to another.

To throw a thicker veil of obscurity over the system, each source of income was classified under a different case or schedule: from schedule A for income from unfurnished lettings, to schedule F for income from dividends. Separate tax rules applied to the different cases and schedules. Some income was taxed on the basis of income arising in that tax year, and some on the basis of income arising in the previous tax year.

Although plans to reform the system are in the pipeline, these rules and classifications still survive. The subdivision of tax offices is, however, now largely obsolete. Tax offices are arranged more for administrative convenience than for the confidentiality originally planned. Some offices deal with specialised areas, such as Pay As You Earn, profit-related pay schemes or the construction industry sub-contractor schemes.

Other offices deal with the day-to-day administration of tax affairs. The most basic division here is between departments dealing with Schedule D (usually self employed income): and Schedule E (income from employment). Schedule D and E departments may be housed in the same building, but communication between the two, as between different tax offices, is often somewhat tortuous.

Which Tax Office?

Which tax office deals with your affairs? These are the points to consider:

- Is my tax office the local office?
- Is my tax office outside the local area?
- Is my tax office a 'special' office?
- Do I have more than one tax office?

The local office

For many people, the tax office is the local tax office – the one physically closest. Tax office boundaries often parallel those of local government by parish or county. Usually there is little ambiguity but, if there is any possible confusion, a quick telephone call to the nearest Revenue office should give you the answer.

Offices further afield

But the nearest office is not always the one dealing with your affairs. Your tax office may be far from local for a variety of reasons:

- The tax office has been relocated. (Where this happens there are usually local enquiry offices left.)
- You work for a firm based in a different area. Your tax office will then usually be that for the area where your employer is based.
- You make claims for repayment of income tax paid on invest-ment income. You may then deal with an office dealing specif-ically with repayment claims.
- You receive a pension from someone based outside your area. Your office is likely to be the one that deals with whoever pays your pension.
- You are a company director, and the company has its regis-tered office elsewhere. Your office is likely to be that dealing with the area where the company is registered.
- You are in business on your own account and have moved. Occasionally, if the move is relatively local, you may still be dealt with by your original tax office.
- You are a partner in a firm and live outside the area in which the firm has its principal place of business. Your tax office is likely to be that dealing with the firm.

More than one tax office?

To add to the confusion, if you have more than one source of income, you may have more than one tax office. There are plans for administrative reorganisation so that the whole of a taxpayer's income will be dealt with by one office. But at present, there are many people whose affairs are dealt with by more than one office. This is likely to be the case where, for example, some-one is self-employed but also has part-time work as an employee; or where someone has a pension and also works part time. In this situation, one office will act nominally as the main tax office, but in practice each office will deal with separate aspects of your affairs. The office nearest you will deal with any self-employment since the income arises from a place of business in its area. The other tax office will be that of your employer or whoever provides your pension.

Who should you speak to?

What sort of problem are you?

One lady of spirit had a notice in her office: 'Have you come with the answer or are you part of the problem?' Who you should speak to at the Revenue depends on what sort of problem you are. Considering what sort of problem you are, from the Revenue's point of view, will help you to get through to the right person.

The grouping below may help you to see your position from the Revenue's point of view:

- Self-employed?
  You are a Schedule D case.
- Just started in business?
  You are a Schedule D 'new case'.
- Employee?
  You are a Schedule E case or a PAYE matter.
- Limited company?
  You are a corporation tax case.
- Other incorporated body?
  You are a corporation tax case.
- Made a one-off gain? (for example, by selling an old picture found in the attic?)
  You are a capital gains tax case. (If you had found a vintage car, you would have been more fortunate. They are not taxable.)
- Investment income your only source of income? All taxed at source?
  You are probably a repayment case.

Your first point of contact

If you phone a tax office, your call will be taken by the switchboard. The person answering your call needs to know who to put you through to. This is where, armed with the classification above, you state the sort of problem you are. Ask for Schedule D or Schedule E. Categorise your enquiry – you can say you have an enquiry about capital gains or a repayment claim, or so on. It also helps to quote your tax reference number.

Tax references

Tax references for employees appear on documents such as the leaving certificate, form P45, or the year-end summary of pay, tax and National Insurance, form P60. The first three numbers of the reference identify the tax office. The following series of digits and letters identify your employer or the provider of your pension. Your National Insurance number makes up the final part of your reference. All self-employed people are allocated a tax reference number when they notify the Revenue that they have started in business. If you are contacting the Revenue to do precisely this, identify yourself as a 'new case' and you will be passed on to someone who can set up a file for you, complete with identifying number. For those who have been in self-employment for some time, the tax reference can be run to earth on tax bills, income tax returns, or correspondence from the Revenue.

Who is at the other end?

Who takes your call depends to some extent on your query. Usually you will only speak to an Inspector if you specifically ask to do so, if your problem is particularly complex or if you are enquiring about capital taxes. If the issue is very involved, it is often best to ask for written confirmation of the points raised. This helps to keep confusion to a minimum, and should lessen the chance of your having to argue after the event with a different Inspector who may take a different view of your problem.

The Revenue's approach to accounts

What happens when your accounts are submitted to the Revenue? How big is the magnifying glass under which the Sherlock Holmes of the Revenue put your figures?

Accepting the figures

If not elementary, the answer to these questions is strongly tempered with practical considerations. The sheer volume of accounts sent in to the Revenue makes it impracticable for all sets of figures to be reviewed in detail. Usually accounts are accepted at face value unless there are obvious mistakes or inconsistencies. This will result in a notice being issued stating that the figures are 'accepted' – the Revenue never 'agrees' accounts. If you have an accountant acting for you, this notice will be sent to him or her. If you prepare your own figures, you should receive this yourself.

If you submit your own figures, it is likely that you will be asked a few questions before the accounts are accepted. This is particularly so if the figures are for your very first year in business. A typical query might relate to the size of any deduction made for wages for your spouse or any member of your family working in your business. The Revenue is always keen to verify that such payments are not inflated beyond a normal commercial level. Another area where the Revenue is likely to be alert is the inclusion of non-allowable expenses such as clothing. Usually only specifically safety wear, such as steel toe-capped boots is allowable. (See Chapter 6.)

In-depth investigations

As part of the process of receiving and accepting accounts, the Revenue will occasionally investigate a taxpayer's affairs in depth. It does not matter that your accounts have been accepted without query for years past; the next set of figures may still be chosen for such investigation.

An in-depth investigation is likely to arise because the Inspector feels that there is something unusual about your affairs. There are many factors which may raise questions in the official mind – and they by no means all relate to your business:

- Your level of private expenses is low.
- There are mistakes or omissions on your accounts or tax return.
- Your accounts are different in some way from those of similar businesses.

- The Inspector has reason to believe that you have another business or have not declared all your income.

During an in-depth investigation, the Inspector is likely to want to see all your business records. He or she may also want to see records of your private income and expenses, such as private bank and savings accounts details. Reviewing these records, the Inspector will want to know the source of money you have received in business and private accounts. You will be expected to be able to substantiate your answers, usually with some written documentary evidence: in the case of a legacy, this might be a letter from the solicitors dealing with the matter, or a bookie's ticket for a win at the races.

The Inspector will normally ask to interview you in person in order to discuss your life-style and business. The issue under scrutiny here is whether you appear to be living in a way that can be supported by the profits you have declared for your business – or whether you seem to have additional business income, perhaps from undisclosed sources. Confessing to a weakness for yachting holidays, fast cars and caviare sandwiches when your business is reporting profits of only £4500 a year is likely to provoke questions. At some stage in the process you may be asked to complete a form which puts a value on all your belongings and quantifies all your debts.

The Inspector has considerable powers when it comes to drawing the investigation to a close. Additional tax bills, and even penalties, can be raised if the Inspector feels that these are appropriate. They may be raised if it is held, for example, that you have insufficient evidence to support a particular deduction from your income (again, payments to members of your family are a prime target), or that you are likely to have received money not declared in your accounts. The penalty can be up to 100 per cent of the additional tax. Penalties can be reduced if you voluntarily disclose that you have had any undeclared income, or that you have over-stated expenses and if you have made every effort to co-operate. The seriousness of the case may also be taken into account in calculating penalties.

Minimising risk

If you are in business, there is always the possibility of an in-depth investigation. The best way to minimise your exposure, if your affairs are selected for investigation, is a policy of accurate and comprehensive record keeping. Maintaining a separate cash book for private expenses is also worth considering. When you send accounts to the Revenue, full disclosure of any unusual or contentious items should also help.

The Revenue year

The tax year begins on 6 April and ends on 5 April the following year.

- 6 April
  Start of tax year
- April
  Income tax returns issued to taxpayers
- 1 July
  Second instalment of annual tax bill due (self-employed people)
- Autumn
  Income tax assessments issued for coming January
- 1 January
  First instalment of annual tax bill due (self-employed people)
- 5 April
  End of tax year

Other dates in the Revenue calendar:

- 19th of each month
  Payment of deductions made from employees' wages by employers
  These sums are normally due 14 days after the end of each tax month. The tax month begins on the 5th of each month
- 30 April
  Inheritance tax due (or six months after the occasion of transfer; closer examination of the rules necessary here)
- 30 September
  Last acceptable date for submission of income tax returns (see Chapter 7)

- 1 December
  Capital gains tax bills due
- Corporation tax
  Companies usually have nine months from their year end to pay tax on their profits. Tax on dividends and interest, however, is paid quarterly
- Other tax bills
  Most other tax is due on 1 January, or 30 days from the date on which the Inspector first issues a demand.

The timescale for action

Most of the forms you receive from the Revenue require some action within 30 days of issue. The date of issue should be marked on the form, and it is this date, rather than the date on which it comes through your letterbox, which is important; the two can differ!

Many Revenue forms will mention the deadlines you will have to work to. But, in some cases, you may need to start things moving yourself. When you are thinking of claiming allowances, pension relief or relief for a loss made in your business, for example, you may need to act fast. The recent election for unconditional transfer of the married couple's allowance has to be made *before* the beginning of the tax year! More usually, claims and elections are on a two-year or a six-year time limit. These would be points to check with the Revenue, a reference publication or with an adviser.

Income tax returns

Income tax returns are sent out at the start of each new tax year to taxpayers for whom the Inland Revenue has files. They go predominantly to self-employed people but employees may receive a tax return, as may people with investment income and pensions.

Strictly speaking, tax returns are supposed to be completed and sent back to the Revenue within 30 days from the date they are issued. In practice, it is usually accepted if the return is submitted before 30 September in each year. If returns are made late, interest may be charged on any tax that is paid late as a result of the delay.

Tax assessments

The timescale for contacting the Revenue is short. Tax assessments require action within 30 days if there is anything which has to be changed. This applies not just to income tax assessments but capital gains tax assessments, and any other tax bills. If there is an error in the figures, you must contact the Revenue. (See Chapter 8.)

The timescale, as far as your own plans and cash flow are concerned, depends to some extent on the time of year that you receive an assessment. If you receive a tax demand in October for payment the following January, you will need to write back within 30 days if you disagree with the figures, but you have almost three months to sort things out. On the other hand, a tax bill raised at almost any other time of the year is unlikely to give you such a lengthy planning horizon, and you may well have to pay out money within 30 days of receiving the bill.

The Revenue writes back

In general, it is unlikely that you will receive a reply from the Revenue in under 14 days. Depending on the Revenue workload, you may often wait longer than this. There are always exceptions but it is worth bearing in mind when you are considering a reminder. A telephone enquiry might make all the difference to speed!

Normal correspondence with the Revenue

The Revenue has a form for most circumstances, and it often helps your affairs to go through more easily if you use the appropriate form.

If you don't have all the information asked for in a Revenue form or don't seem to fit the category, don't be afraid to write 'not applicable' or to send a covering letter of explanation. Sending the form in will get things moving, allow a file to be set up or let a job progress to the next stage. It is always wise to keep a copy of everything you send in: photocopies or carbon copies are best but a handwritten copy will do. This way you can follow developments and check up on what needs to be done next.

Standard forms

- 41 G   Notifies Revenue of start of self-employment
- 41 K   Can be used to submit 'simple tax accounts' for businesses with turnover of less than £15,000
- 300 CODA   Tax assessment
- 329 CODA   Tax assessment issued to partnership
- 64–7   Form used to appeal and/or postpone a tax assessment
- 64–4 (1)   Agreement to an appeal and postponement
- 64–8   Appoints agent to act for you, and authorises Revenue to send copy assessments to agent
- 46 A   Acceptance of accounts submitted
- R40 (SP) (OCR)   Tax repayment claim for tax deducted from investment income
- P1   Income tax return
- P45   Leaving certificate issued to employees
- P60   End of year certificate issued to employees showing tax and salary paid
- 715   Certificate issued by sub-contractor in construction industry, authorising payment without deduction of 25 per cent tax
- 714   Identifying certificate with photo held by sub-contractor in construction industry allowing him or her to issue 715s

Unusual circumstances

Now you know what to expect in the normal run of events but what happens when things go wrong?

One of the most unusual aspects of the current income tax regime is that you are sometimes taxed in arrears on what you earned last year, and sometimes taxed on what you are earning now. This usually works reasonably smoothly but getting into, or out of, the system can cause problems. This can happen in the following circumstances:

- Setting up in business
- Finishing self-employment
- Receiving income from rented property

Setting up in business

When you start self-employment, you may find that the Revenue estimate your profits almost as soon as you have finished the first year's trading, and send you an assessment. This is partly a pre-cautionary measure on their part, to remind taxpayers new to self-employment that they have to send in figures. Be warned, and try to make up your first set of accounts as soon as possible. Usually it is best to wait until you have been trading for at least 12 months.

Finishing self-employment

When you stop being self employed, it is again time to contact the Revenue. Until they are notified that you are no longer in busi-ness, they are likely to carry on taxing you on a preceding year basis. This means that you may be taxed on 12 months' profit even though you may have been trading for only a few months during that tax year. In the final set of calculations before your self-employed file is laid to rest, there is the possibility that the tax bills for two years previously will be revised by the Revenue. This may result in an additional bill.

Rental income

Rental income from property is taxed in the year you earn it. The tax bills are due on 1 January and are based on your income from 6 April the year before, to 5 April following. What happens if your tenant moves out on 1 December? Your January tax bill will be based on your rental income as though your tenant had stayed until 5 April. It is up to you to do something: if you tell the Revenue what has happened, and if you don't expect to re-let the property that tax year, the figures can be revised.

When do you need to get in touch?

Change of circumstances

- You become entitled to a new allowance
- You cease to be entitled to an allowance currently claimed
- You are divorced, married or separated

- You take out a pension or increase pension payments
- You first start to receive a pension
- You let out a house for the first time
- You stop letting out a house
- You move away from your main private residence on which you have a mortgage
- You begin self-employment
- You receive a new source of income which is not taxed

When you need to make a claim

- For loss relief in your business
- To transfer the married couple's allowance
- To claim tax relief on a pension in earlier years (relating back)
- To claim capital gains tax roll-over relief when you sell a business or business assets and then buy another business or business assets

3. Dealing with VAT

Who are Customs and Excise?

Customs and Excise administer Value Added Tax (VAT). Their operation is completely different from the Inland Revenue. Customs and Excise have long been used to catching smugglers, checking distilleries and the sort of activities which seem to spring from the pages of *Whisky Galore*. The precision with which VAT is managed shows all the marks of such a background: VAT operates to extraordinarily clearly defined rules. High up in the VAT hierarchy, the hairs of taxation are split. Decisions are taken as to what constitutes public transport – and whether hot air balloons can provide it – and whether biscuit tins are products separate from the biscuits inside.

What are they looking for?

The accuracy with which these distinctions are made is worth bearing in mind, for this is the order of accuracy expected from the trader registered for VAT.

VAT is a tax on final consumers and non-VAT registered businesses. For VAT purposes, all services and products are classified into three groups:

- Standard rated taxable products
- Zero rated taxable products
- Exempt products

VAT is currently charged at 17.5 per cent on standard rated products; on zero rated taxable products it is charged at 0 per cent. Exempt products are outside the scope of VAT.

These groupings are the key to VAT. If you are a business and what you sell is taxable – even if it is zero rated, and taxed at 0 per cent – you can usually reclaim the VAT on products and services that you buy for your business. If part of what you sell is exempt, you cannot reclaim all the VAT on what you buy.

Businesses which are registered for VAT have two roles as far as Customs and Excise are concerned. They have a tax-collecting role: they collect on behalf of Customs and Excise the VAT charged on the products and services they sell. And they also have an accounting role, distinguishing and balancing the VAT charged to them on products bought for business use, and the VAT they charge on their own products and services.

Essentially, VAT registered businesses are dealing with tax-payers' money; Customs and Excise are there to check that the collection of this money is carried out correctly, and that VAT is properly isolated from other business receipts.

Role of Customs and Excise
- To check that products and services are classified correctly
- To check that the rate of tax used is correct
- To check that deductions for the use of products in the business are valid
- To check that the detail of the rules has been applied

The concern of Customs and Excise is therefore that VAT registered businesses have adequate accounting records. VAT registered businesses must be able to account clearly for all money received, and show how figures for the amount of tax payable to Customs and Excise – or the amount reclaimed from them – have been calculated.

Voluntary registration

Businesses with a turnover over a certain level (from 1 December 1993, £45,000 for 12 months) are required to register for VAT by law. Businesses with a lower level of turnover may choose to register for VAT on a voluntary basis as long as Customs and

Excise are happy that what they do counts as business, and is not, for example, a hobby. There are a number of factors which may affect the decision about whether or not to register voluntarily:

In favour of voluntary registration

- *Buying more cheaply*
  If you buy from VAT registered businesses, the services and products you buy will be cheaper. They will only cost you the figure before VAT is charged – the 'net' figure.
- *Confidentiality*
  No one will know the size of your business. If you are not registered, it is obvious that your turnover is below the registration limit.
- *Business confidence*
  You may want the appearance of being a well-established business. VAT registration may enhance your presentation.
- *Avoiding VAT penalties*
  If your turnover is already close to the compulsory registration limit, you can avoid the possibility of incurring penalties for registering at the wrong date.
- *Improved cash flow*
  Properly managed, VAT will improve your cash flow. Your gross income may increase by up to 17.5 per cent, and you may receive refunds.
- *Reducing the cost of expensive capital equipment*
  On every £10,000 of equipment (before tax) there is £1750 of VAT. If you are registered, you receive a rebate of the £1750 on most items. (There are certain exceptions, such as cars. The small print of VAT legislation should be looked into here.)

Points against registration

- *Record keeping*
  You will need to keep more extensive records.
- *VAT returns*
  You will need to prepare a return to Customs and Excise, usually every three months. There is also an annual scheme which is suitable for some businesses. Returns here are only made once in 12 months. Some businesses, which usually receive refunds, prepare a return each month.

- *Penalty regime*
  If your cash flow gets out of control, and payments to Customs
  and Excise are made late, you will have to pay penalties. There
  is no penalty for the first offence, but continuing problems will
  incur penalties.
- *Errors on VAT returns*
  If you make an error on a VAT return, even by accident, you
  may be penalised.
- *Selling to the public*
  If you supply the general public rather than other VAT registered businesses, your products and services will be more
  expensive by 17.5 per cent, as the consumer has to pay your
  price plus VAT.

When do you have to get in touch?

There are two main occasions when you need to contact Customs
and Excise:

- If you are not already registered for VAT and exceed the registration limits for turnover.
- If you are registered for VAT and discover an error on your
  VAT return which is more than the limits where you are
  allowed to make an adjustment yourself.

Registration limits

Registration limits are usually increased each year. The current
limit (from 1 December 1993) is £45,000. If your turnover
exceeds this level over the previous 12 months, you must inform
Customs and Excise and apply for registration. The time limit for
notification here is 30 days from the end of the month in which
you went over the turnover limit.

You may also have to register if you *expect* that your turnover
will exceed £45,000 in the 30 days coming. This could be the case
if, for example, you are organising an event such as a fair or
auction which is to take place on a particular day or for a particular week.

There are severe penalties if you do not notify Customs and
Excise at the correct time. For non-VAT registered businesses,

constant vigilance is required. If you are close to the registration limit, turnover levels will have to be checked each month.

Disclosing errors

If you find an error of £1000 or under on your VAT return, you can adjust it yourself on your next return. The March 1993 Budget Notes indicate that this limit will in future be £2000 but as late as November 1993 returns are still being sent out printed with the old limit.

For errors greater than this, you need to inform your regional VAT office. If you leave errors to be discovered by VAT officials, you may have to pay penalties and interest on any amounts due to Customs and Excise.

In addition to contact on registration or disclosure of errors, there are a number of other occasions on which you may contact the VAT office. These include:

- In a case of uncertainty, to check whether you should charge VAT on any particular item.
- If you think there may be any doubt about how your circumstances should be interpreted, to ask for an official ruling: this could happen where you are involved in a number of different business ventures and need to know which are included under your VAT registration, for instance.
- If you think you have been charged VAT incorrectly on any product you have purchased.
- If you think you may have difficulty paying VAT due to Customs and Excise at the end of a return period.
- If your business circumstances change, for example, you take a partner, become a limited company, sell your business or start a new one.
- If you change your name or address.

Getting started

Whether you register because you choose to do so, or because you have to do so, the procedure is the same – and fairly speedy. When you have decided that you need to register, just telephone your local VAT office for the registration forms. These are straightforward to complete, and within about ten days of returning them you should be notified of your VAT registration number. The registration number should be included on all the sales documents you raise after your registration date. Useful points to bear in mind at this early stage are:

- Order relevant VAT leaflets and read them. This will make sure that you start off on an informed footing.
- Life is simpler if your VAT return quarters coincide with your accounting year end. This will not be done automatically but you can ask to be given particular VAT quarters. If you don't do so when you register, you can still ask to change at a later date.
- If you use a computerised accounting system, check that it is acceptable to Customs and Excise. If you are in retail trade, check that it will enable you to operate the retail scheme you have chosen. Can it provide any other details specific to your business, as well as the basic information needed for VAT returns?
- Think about the cash accounting scheme. You can join this scheme as soon as you register if your turnover is below £350,000 per annum. If you give significant periods of credit on your sales, the scheme is likely to assist your cash flow. Under the scheme you pay the VAT you collect to Customs and Excise only when you receive it; otherwise it becomes due to Customs and Excise as soon as you raise a VAT invoice.
- Think about the annual accounting scheme. To be eligible, you have to be registered for at least 12 months. With this scheme, you make a return only once in 12 months.
- Review your accounting records and procedures. Proper accounting records for VAT may go far beyond those required to produce your accounts. Inadequate records produce inaccurate returns – and inaccurate returns are likely to prove expensive. The following list details the type of information you may need readily to hand:
  - Total monthly and quarterly sales, excluding VAT
  - Total monthly and quarterly purchases, excluding VAT
  - The engine capacity and monthly business mileage of your vehicle. In order to calculate the appropriate fuel scale

charge, you need to be able to substantiate your business mileage if it is more than 1500 miles each month, 4500 miles each quarter
- Monthly and quarterly VAT on goods and services supplied and used by your business
- Details of private use of business assets
- Details of your own consumption of business stock
- Details of workings showing how the figures on your VAT return are calculated
- Reconciliation of your turnover between turnover shown on your accounts and turnover shown on VAT returns. (These are not always the same for a variety of reasons.)

Routine inspection visits

Inspection visits are routine with Customs and Excise. You are likely to be visited within the first three years of registration. You may not then receive another visit for years, or you may be visited more frequently. Much depends on the size of your business and the standard of your record keeping.

The VAT officer who is to visit you will contact you in advance to set up an appointment. You will usually be asked to have all your business records available for inspection. These include:

- Your business bank statements, used cheque books and paying-in books
- Your cash book
- Sales and purchase ledgers if you use them
- Your sales and purchase invoices
- Your accounts, together with a reconciliation of turnover between your accounts and VAT returns
- Copies of your VAT returns
- Your workings showing how the figures on VAT returns are made up
- Your VAT registration certificate
- Agreements to put you on any schemes, such as the cash accounting scheme
- Details of calculations if you are on a special retail scheme
- Any special records required to operate a second-hand scheme

- Any correspondence you have had with Customs and Excise
- Any relevant business correspondence

The Inspector will then review your records. If any errors are discovered, they will be identified and you will be advised about what action you need to take. Should you disagree with the Inspector, you will be advised of your rights of appeal. It is important not to leave disclosure of any errors that you may have discovered yourself until you are visited. Make a note and adjust them as soon as you become aware of them. If they are over the level where self-adjustment is permitted, write to Customs and Excise. If you have any queries about the way that specific items should be treated for VAT purposes, and have not previously asked Customs and Excise for their opinion, you can use this opportunity to ask the Inspector for advice.

Your VAT return

Once you are registered for VAT, you will need to complete a VAT return, usually every three months. If you are due repayments, you may choose to make monthly returns in order to improve your cash flow.

The return will be sent to you during the last month of the quarter. This means that if you make your returns to 30 June, 30 September, 31 December and 31 March, your forms will arrive towards the end of those months. You will then have until the end of July, October, January and April to complete and send in the return, together with the appropriate payment.

If you are due a refund, Customs and Excise will normally pay it within 30 days of receiving your return. If you regularly receive returns, the refund will be sent to your bank by automated credit.

Accuracy and timeliness are vital. If your return has arithmetical errors, or boxes are not completed, problems will follow. If you are due a refund, Customs and Excise will not process it, and if you are due to make a payment, they may estimate the bill for you. The estimate is payable and will only be adjusted once the return has been completed correctly.

You will be sent a prepaid envelope with your return. Do not lose it; it is stamped with specific references, and sending in your return in a different envelope may lead to delay in processing the return. If such a delay takes you outside the time limits for submission, penalties could accrue. All monthly and quarterly VAT returns are sent to the VAT Central Unit at Southend, and not to local VAT enquiry offices.

The quarterly VAT return is your main contact with Customs and Excise. The only other returns you are likely to make cover situations such as registration, de-registration, changes in business circumstances and notification of errors. These would be addressed to your local VAT office.

VAT vocabulary
- Inputs
  The value of goods and services bought by your business, excluding VAT.
- Outputs
  The value of goods and services sold by your business, excluding VAT.
- Input tax
  VAT you can reclaim from Customs and Excise on goods and services used in your business.
- Output tax
  VAT you charge to your customers on the goods and services you provide.

Key points in preparing a return

- Always keep a copy of your return.
- Keep a copy of your workings showing how the figures on the return are made up.
- Check that your figures make sense. If everything you sell is standard rated, the output tax on your sales should be 17.5 per cent of the total outputs. If it isn't, there's an error. You can't do exactly the same check on purchases, or zero rated sales, but using the same principle you can see if the figures look reasonable.
- Double check your arithmetic – especially if you are on a retail

scheme. An arithmetically incorrect return will be rejected by Customs and Excise, even if you have simply transposed two figures when copying your input or output tax from your workings and the refund or payment calculated is still correct.

- Don't rely on computers – a quick manual check often identifies small bugs in the system or errors in keying in.
- Reconcile your returns to the accounts as soon as you can. If you are asked to do so in three years' time, it may prove a great deal more difficult.
- Ask someone else to review your workings. Even if this happens only occasionally, it will give you confidence and share the responsibility.
- If you are in any doubt about how to treat any transaction, ask for advice. The phone number of your VAT office is on the front of your return, so there's no excuse!
- Keep up to date with paperwork. Do as much work in advance as you can. If you analyse all the figures in your cash book properly as you go along, there will only be one month to add on when you reach a quarter end.
- Adjust any errors that you have discovered in previous returns if £1000 or less. (The March 1993 Budget indicates a future limit of £2000.)
- Notify Customs and Excise of errors over £1000.
- Remember that tax you pay to Customs and Excise is not input tax. Exclude it from your figures before you prepare your return.
- Remember to make adjustments for private use of business assets (cars, computers, etc) and to show these clearly on your workings.
- Make sure that you include VAT payable on goods for own consumption.
- Reclaiming input tax on fuel? Remember to include a fuel scale charge where you reclaim input tax on fuel used in vehicles also used for non-business purposes.
- Business assets sold? If you have sold business fittings, equipment or vehicles (other than private cars), you must charge VAT on the sale: 7/47 of whatever you receive is payable to Customs and Excise. Add this to your output tax.
- Financial difficulties? If you are likely to have trouble paying

any VAT due, get in touch with Customs and Excise at once and explain why. Use a secure method of payment. If you are worried about your bank honouring a cheque, remember that Customs and Excise will no longer re-present cheques that bounce. This could mean that you will need to pay in cash at your local VAT office, or send a banker's draft or postal order to Southend. Delay could lead to financial penalties.

- Repayment due? If you are due a repayment, the sooner you send in your return, the sooner you are likely to get the cheque in your hands.
- If you have received any credit notes from your suppliers, make sure that you deduct any VAT shown from your input tax.
- Check your purchase invoices. Don't reclaim VAT as input tax unless you have a valid VAT invoice. This should show:
  - Date
  - Your name and address
  - Supplier's name, address and VAT number
  - Description of the goods bought
  - Rate of tax charged, and amount of VAT included (or state that the total figure includes VAT at 17.5 per cent)
  - Simplified rules apply to small retail sales
  - Other details will be found in the *VAT Guide* in the section on tax invoices.

Timescale for action

Most of the forms you receive from the VAT office will specify the time limits you must work to.

With a normal VAT return, you effectively have a little under a month to prepare the figures. You can't start before your quarter end unless you are absolutely certain that there will be no more transactions to record. If you are not on the cash scheme, you may need to wait a few weeks after the quarter end to receive all the necessary invoices from your suppliers. As the return and your payment must reach Customs and Excise before the end of the month – and must be correct – this can be a tight timescale. Any planning you can do in advance will help.

As regards most other matters, VAT works in 'real time'. All transactions, once made, are fixed, and will be interpreted by Customs and Excise in only one way. They are unlikely to permit a variety of interpretations, or any adjustments, after the event. For these reasons, if you come across any transaction which you are in doubt about how to treat, it is best to ask. Errors can be avoided; they are less easily corrected after the event.

The catch 22 is that to have any idea of what the problem areas are, you need to know quite a lot about VAT. Some of these areas are highlighted below as pitfalls.

Pitfalls to avoid

One guide to expensive VAT pitfalls comes from a review of the recent decisions of the VAT tribunal. This is the appeal body which hears cases where the Commissioners of Customs and Excise and business people cannot reach agreement. Problems frequently arise from the type of areas listed below:

- *Timing*
  When timing is critical in the submission of returns, use registered post or recorded delivery.
- *VAT invoices*
  - Do not reclaim input tax before you have the VAT invoice.
  - Check the dates shown on your purchase invoices and make sure that you do not reclaim any VAT prematurely.
  - Make sure that purchase invoices are in the right name, especially if you have a number of different business activities.
- *Record keeping*
  Make sure that your record keeping is adequate even before you register for VAT. Poor records could leave you open to a challenge of under-stated turnover, and then a penalty for late registration.
- *Construction*
  Watch zero rating on property. This is particularly relevant where an older building is only partly demolished before being incorporated into a new residence. Only limited classes of domestic and charitable buildings are now zero rated, and these must be built 'new' – not by 'repairing' an old building.

- *Not on the cash scheme?*
  If you are not on the cash scheme, and still prefer to account for VAT only when you receive the sales monies due, make sure that you understand the use of pro forma invoices properly. A pro forma invoice is a request for payment: it is not a VAT invoice, and must state 'This is not a VAT invoice'. If you require customers to pay to pro forma invoices, you should issue a VAT invoice only when you have received payment. If you receive a pro forma invoice, you cannot recover the VAT paid using the pro forma. You must wait until you receive a VAT invoice.
- *Attributable supplies*
  Watch the principle of attributable supplies. This means that in order to reclaim input tax on a particular item, you must be able to show that you have used that input item to make a taxable supply. The consequence is that if, for example, you make any sales which are exempt from VAT, you will be unable to reclaim tax on inputs used in the process of making those sales.
- *No VAT can be reclaimed on*
  - Cars, other than driving school cars, taxis and self-drive hire cars
  - Business entertainment
  - Items bought for personal or non-business use
  - Postage stamps.

Penalties

Since the Finance Act 1993, the major VAT penalties are now as follows:

- Serious misdeclaration penalty
- Persistent misdeclaration penalty
- Default surcharge

Serious misdeclaration penalty

Who is at risk?

This is designed to penalise traders who do not pay all the VAT due, or who overstate claims for repayment of VAT. However, the rules penalise innocent errors as much as errors made deliberately.

There are grounds for appeal, and opportunities for mitigation, but it is much the best policy to ensure that your procedures are reliable and accurate. If you do find an error in your records, you may avoid penalties by voluntarily disclosing it.

The size of error

Small errors are ignored. The penalty regime defines a serious error as one that exceeds 30 per cent of the 'relevant amount of tax'. In addition, larger companies make a serious error when the error is more than £1 million.

In most circumstances, the relevant amount of tax is the gross amount of tax. This is the total of your input tax and output tax added together. Different rules apply if Customs and Excise estimate a return for you, which proves to be an underestimate, and you do not take action on it within 30 days. A stricter test then applies.

A Customs and Excise press release on 10 March 1992 indicated that a penalty will not normally be imposed where the error amounts to £2000 or under.

The size of penalty

In official parlance the penalty is equal to 15 per cent of the size of the error – in other words you are charged 15 per cent of the sum lost to Customs and Excise. This is, of course, in addition to paying the tax due to correct your original error – and interest may also be due.

Persistent misdeclaration penalty

Who is at risk?

This penalty was introduced to penalise people making errors smaller than those described above but who keep doing so. It is imposed only after a number of errors have been made and discovered by Customs and Excise, and after a 'notice of liability' to penalties has been issued by them. Again, there are appeal and mitigation procedures, and voluntary disclosure may avoid penalties.

The size of error

To be considered here, an error must be at least 10 per cent of the gross amount of tax. In addition, for larger companies, errors over £500,000 are also relevant and are termed 'material' errors.

Procedure

A penalty liability notice may be served after the discovery of one material error. The penalty liability notice sets out a timescale within which you are liable to penalties. It runs for the period covered by your next eight VAT returns. If you make an error in your second or subsequent return, a penalty at the rate of 15 per cent may be imposed. The tax overclaimed or underpaid must also be paid.

Default surcharge

Who is at risk?

Default surcharge is possibly the most likely form of penalty that a trader registered for VAT will meet. It is imposed for late submission of returns and failure to pay money due by the correct date. If your return and payment arrive late, notice of liability will be issued before penalties are imposed.

Procedure and penalties

A surcharge liability notice may be issued when a return or payment arrives with Customs and Excise after the due date. The notice will set out how long your 'surcharge liability period' will last. This is usually for a year. If during this time another return or payment arrives late, you will be liable for a penalty. In addition, your liability period may also be extended. Customs and Excise have indicated that they may not charge penalties where the amount due is under £200 and a first offence. A sliding scale of penalties applies, with a minimum penalty of £30:

- First default in liability period
  2 per cent of tax which should have been paid to Customs and Excise and was not paid by the correct date
- Second default in liability period
  5 per cent of tax
- Third default in liability period
  10 per cent of tax
- Fourth and following defaults in liability period
  15 per cent of tax

Interest and other penalties

There is a wide range of other penalties imposed for breach of regulations, civil fraud, late registration for VAT, errors on EC sales statements, tax evasion and other misdemeanours.

4. Your National Insurance and benefits

The Benefits and Contributions Agencies: who are they?

These two bodies are executive agencies of the Department of Social Security. As their titles suggest, the Benefits Agency deals with social security payments to you; the Contributions Agency with payments made by you.

What are they looking for?

The key to identity, as far as the DSS is concerned, is your National Insurance number. Provided with the magic number, staff will be able to access your records for you. How to find a lost number is outlined above, on page 19.

Dealing with the Benefits Agency?

The range of social security benefits which self-employed people can claim is somewhat restricted. If you are self-employed, therefore, your dealings with the Benefits Agency are likely to be limited. Statutory sick pay is the benefit most likely to be of relevance. People who are self-employed are entitled to a basic rate of sick pay, and are not liable to make the usual flat rate contributions while off work because of illness. There is no entitlement to unemployment benefit.

For employees, there may be more contact with the Agency.

Employees who pay National Insurance are entitled to a wider range of benefits than the self-employed.

Contributions Agency: when do you need to get in touch?

* Starting self-employment
* Finishing self-employment
* Asking about National Insurance contributions
* Applying for an exception from Class 2
* Applying for a refund of Class 2
* Checking your liability to pay Class 2
* Deferring contributions
* Applying to make voluntary National Insurance contributions

Starting self-employment

Contact your local Contributions Agency when you become self-employed. The Agency will issue a form for you to complete. This enables the Agency to trace your previous National Insurance record (if any), and set up a file for your Class 2 self-employed contributions.

Finishing self-employment

It is up to you get in touch so that your final National Insurance liability can be worked out. This should mean that you are not chased to pay for any weeks when you were not self-employed.

Asking about National Insurance

Employer or employee? – your contributions

Most employees and most employers will have few occasions to contact the DSS. Liability and collection are arranged via the Pay As You Earn (PAYE) system organised by the Inland Revenue. Employees and employers pay Class 1 National Insurance contributions. Employers may also be liable to pay Class 1A contributions on taxable benefits provided for employees.

Employed and self employed?

There are special rules if you are self-employed as well as working as an employee. You may have to make self-employed contributions as well as your contributions as an employee. You could be liable to pay Class 2 and Class 4 contributions as well as Class 1.

Self-employed?

Self-employed people are liable to pay two types of National Insurance: Class 2 and Class 4.

Class 2 contributions are flat-rate contributions. In the year from 6 April 1994 these are £5.65 per week. Where turnover is below certain limits, it is possible to be exempted from Class 2. The procedure is explained below.

Class 4 contributions are profit-related and are usually calculated by the Inland Revenue. From 6 April 1994, the rate of Class 4 contributions will increase to 7.3 per cent. They are charged on profits between £6490 and £22,360. There is a maximum amount of Class 4 contributions that can be paid. In 1994–95 this is £1158.50. One half of Class 4 contributions constitute an allowable expense, and can be set off against business profits. This is usually done automatically by the Revenue when a tax assessment is raised. The deduction is sometimes shown as 'personal reliefs' here. Class 2 contributions, however, are not tax deductible in this way and no relief is given. An example of how to calculate Class 4 contributions is shown below:

Benjamin Franklin, a self-employed song-writer, has profits of £19,706. His Class 4 bill is calculated as:

	£
Taxable profits	19,706
Lower limit for Class 4	6,490
Profits liable to Class 4	13,216
Class 4 payable at 7.3%	£964.77

Note: £482 (50 per cent of £964.77) is a deduction from profits charged to income tax.

What do you pay?
- Class 2 [1994–95]
  Flat rate, £5.65 per week
  Payable monthly or quarterly
- Class 4 [1994–95]
  At 7.3% on profits between £6490 and £22,360
  Paid with income tax bills, January and July

When do you pay?

When you start to pay Class 2 contributions, you will be given a choice of payment methods, each with its own timetable. You can pay by direct debit each month from a bank or building society account, or you can pay a quarterly bill sent to you direct by the DSS after each 13-week period. (The old method of buying weekly stamps for a contributions card is no longer available.)

Is there any way out?

In some situations, you may not be liable for National Insurance contributions. This is particularly relevant in the following circumstances:

- If you have low profits from part-time self-employment
- If you have a certificate of exception

Low profits

If your annual self-employed profits are low, the Contributions Agency may decline to set up a record for contributions. If your profits are below about £800, and you are also employed and pay Class 1 contributions, you are likely to fall into this category. If you are in business with a partner, this limit is per partner. However, it is important to approach the Contributions Agency and let it make the decision.

Bear in mind that, if profits increase, you may have to start paying National Insurance. If profits are still below a certain level, you may have to apply for a certificate of exception.

Certificates of exception

Who can apply? If you are in business and your annual profits are below a certain level, it is possible to obtain a certificate of exception which exempts you from paying Class 2. The profit threshold is usually changed each year: in 1994–95, it stands at £3200. Should you run your business as a partnership, any partner whose share of profit is under this level may be eligible.

Should you apply? There are both advantages and disadvantages in holding an exception. The main advantage is obvious: you have fewer expenses. This may be especially helpful in the early days of a new business. The disadvantage is that you are not building up a contributions record, and so may be jeopardising your chance of claiming state benefits in the future.

These are points that you may want to weigh up carefully in the light of your plans for the future. It may be that missing a few years' contributions now, in order to put your all into the business, makes more sense to you in terms of cash flow. The contributions can be made up voluntarily at a later stage, but you may then have to pay at a higher rate. Looked at in this way, an exception can be used as a tool to help build up your business. On the other hand, if the future seems more uncertain, and you do not necessarily intend to remain in self-employment for a number of years, access to state benefits may be more important to you.

How and when to apply. Forward thinking is needed as exception claims are made in advance. Certificates will rarely be backdated, and usually for only 13 weeks at most.

To apply for a certificate, contact the Contributions Agency. You will be sent the standard application form, 'People with small earnings from self-employment' (NI27A). This asks you for details of the business, and what level of earnings you expect for the coming year. You will also be asked to provide confirmation of your profits for the previous year. There are a number of ways in which you can provide evidence of your profits. A set of the relevant accounts, the income tax assessment raised on the basis of these figures or a letter from your accountant are all acceptable.

Once your application is processed, you will be sent a certificate of exception which will run for a period of two to three years. It should be kept in a safe place as it will be needed to renew the exception in due course. The DSS should contact you again automatically when it is due to expire. At this point, the performance can be repeated.

Should your profits have risen over the exception threshold in the meantime, the exception becomes invalid. This means that you immediately start to be liable to pay Class 2 contributions.

The exception need not run its full course if you change your mind. You can ask to pay Class 2 contributions or you may choose to make voluntary (Class 3) contributions at any stage.

If you have not obtained a certificate of exception, you may be entitled to obtain a refund of Class 2 if you later discover that your earnings were under the exception threshold. This has only been possible since April 1988.

There are strict time limits for making a refund claim. A claim must be made by 31 December after the end of the relevant tax year. For the tax year ending 5 April 1993, for example, the deadline would be 31 December 1993. It may be difficult to provide confirmation of earnings within the time allowed. This is especially true if you have an accounting year end in the last quarter of the tax year: say, December onwards. In these circumstances, you will not have a set of accounts to use as evidence of profits, and may have to use your accounting records themselves.

The earnings figure you will need for a refund claim is calculated by allocating your profits to the actual tax year. This runs from 6 April in one year to 5 April in the next. So if your accounts are made up to 30 June each year, the 'earnings' figure for the tax year 6 April 1993 to 5 April 1994 would be:

3/12 × year ended 30 June 1993 *plus*
9/12 × year ended 30 June 1994.

Checking your liability to pay Class 2

If you are in one of the following categories, you may escape liability for Class 2.

- If you receive sickness or invalidity benefit
- If you receive unemployability supplement or invalid care allowance
- If you are incapable of work
- If you are in prison or kept in legal custody
- If you are of pensionable age
- If you are under 16

You must fulfil these conditions for a whole contributions week. The contributions week begins on Sunday but the Sunday can be ignored. If for religious reasons you have a different day off and work on Sunday, you ignore the non-working day instead. To have your Class 2 bill adjusted under these circumstances:

- If you pay Class 2 by quarterly bill, enter the details on the form on the back of the quarterly bill sent to you by the DSS. The DSS can then adjust the size of the payment demanded.
- If you pay by direct debit, contact the Class 2 Group of the Contributions Agency whose address can be found on any correspondence you receive from them. If in any doubt, try the direct debit helpline. Its number will also be found here.

Deferring Class 4 or Class 2 contributions

In some circumstances, it is possible to defer making Class 4 or Class 2 contributions. This is especially relevant to people who are employed and self-employed. There is a maximum amount of National Insurance that anyone has to pay in a single year. Paying National Insurance as you go along in a job and also for a self-employed business, it is possible to go over this maximum. Until the end of the tax year, there would be some uncertainty about exactly how much National Insurance would be due.

This is where a Class 4 deferment may be granted. A deferment means that Class 4 will not be charged in the usual way – with the January and July instalments of income tax. Instead, if there is any liability to pay Class 4 once all the calculations are done at the end of the year, it is billed separately.

Deferment is not given automatically – it is something you must apply for, contacting the DSS and stating your reasons.

Application should be made before the beginning of the tax year. In some circumstances, an exemption from Class 4 may be given but deferment is more usual.

Maximum liability

If you are employed and self-employed, the maximum amount of National Insurance you can be liable to pay is:

- full year of Class 2 self-employed contributions *plus*
- the maximum level of Class 1 employee contributions

The actual calculation of how much Class 4 you owe is complex. It involves a comparison of the National Insurance you have paid plus the Class 4 contributions due, with the maximum possible level of contributions. Overall, you may still have to pay Class 1 and Class 4, in addition to Class 2 payments, but the combined total cannot be more than the maximum possible for an employee.

You can also apply to defer paying Class 2 contributions if you are likely to pay more than a certain level of Class 1 employee contributions during the tax year. In 1994–95 the relevant level for deferring Class 4 contributions is £1458.

Applying to make voluntary National Insurance contributions

It is possible to make voluntary National Insurance contributions, regardless of your liability to pay. These payments are called Class 3 contributions. They are charged at £5.55 per week in the year from 6 April 1994. Class 3 contributions may be made, for example, to keep up your rights to a state retirement pension. The Contributions Agency is quite used to people making voluntary contributions, and will sometimes send people who have an exception an invitation to do so. To get things moving, phone your local agency.

5. Keeping records

Records for business

Everyone in business needs records. Records can pay their way, enabling you to prepare accurate accounts, and accurate accounts mean that you can control your business.

Records you have to keep

These are some records that you are required to keep. What they are depends on who you are.

- *Limited companies*
  Limited companies are required to keep certain records by law. The Companies Acts direct that they keep a range of records, from registers of directors and secretaries to accounting records and details of mortgages.
- *VAT registered traders*
  VAT registered traders are also governed by law. They are obliged to keep copies of their VAT account, notes of private use of business goods, and details of gifts or loans of goods and other details in addition to their normal accounting records.
- *All businesses*
  As far as income tax and corporation tax are concerned, the requirement is that a business keep records which will enable accurate accounts to be drawn up.
- *Businesses with employees*
  A business with employees will be required to keep PAYE records.

For most purposes, it is clear what records are insisted on. The law also spells out what can happen if a business fails to comply by setting up penalty regimes. A company which fails to keep at its registered office a register of its directors and secretaries for the inspection of company members, for example, commits an offence. If convicted summarily, it could be fined up to £5000. VAT registered traders who fail to maintain and preserve their VAT records also face a penalty – a £500 fine.

Accounting records

Whatever other specific records are required, all businesses need accounting records. If you are neither a VAT registered trader nor a limited company, the law gives only general guidance about what is necessary. A full set of accounting records will cover these requirements. But what is the best policy for many small businesses which do not find it possible to maintain such a comprehensive system?

A full set of books

The accounting records usually regarded as making up a full set of books can be kept in bound books or on computer. They comprise:

- Cash book and petty cash book
- Purchase and sales day books
- Purchase and sales ledgers
- Nominal ledger, including fixed asset register

These would be supported by:

- Bank records: statements, paying-in books, cheque book stubs
- Copies of sales invoices, purchase invoices and delivery notes
- Copies of loan, HP and other financing agreements
- Copy of the VAT account and returns
- Copies of financial accounts: trading profit and loss account and balance sheet

A full set of accounting books provides an overall picture of business transactions. The books record details of goods and services bought and sold each day, and tell you whether transactions were taken on credit or paid by cash or cheque. They provide information on assets and liabilities as well as supplying an historical record of how the business is performing.

The books listed above are maintained using the double entry system of bookkeeping. Double entry bookkeeping is a sophisticated technique which has developed since the days of the merchants of the Middle Ages. It enables businesses to record every conceivable type of transaction and forms the basis of accounting records. The main advantages of the system are:

- It is self-balancing
- In-built controls check accuracy
- It builds up a complete picture of the business
- It provides a balanced set of books as the starting point to prepare accounts
- It records everything

Recording everything and more

Accounting records based on the double entry system are designed to cope with every type of transaction into which a business can enter. The unique system of debits and credits looks at every transaction from two angles, and provides a remarkable degree of flexibility in recording. It is something of an art to learn. The following example of a day-to-day business transaction looked at with the eye of double entry gives an insight into the way it works.

Benjamin Franklin, candle maker and song-writer, drives into town and fills up his car with petrol. The petrol costs £15 and is charged to his account with the garage.

The transaction of buying petrol has two sides. On the one hand, Benjamin Franklin has more petrol in his car; on the other hand, he now has a liability to pay the garage some money at the end of the month. Written formally, the £15 expense on petrol put into the car is a £15 debit: the £15 liability to pay the garage at the end of the month is a £15 credit.

Despite its great accuracy and flexibility, there are many businesses in which the double entry system is not used, largely because of lack of training or the sheer complexity of the recording needed. To record an entire day of Benjamin Franklin's life in double entry would be an enormously elaborate matter.

Many businesses, therefore, have records which enter only a part of the full transactions. Benjamin Franklin himself, for example, probably only records, at the end of the month, the money spent on petrol, not the day-to-day liability to the garage. He may record the payment from his bank account but is unlikely to have a cumulative record of fuel purchased.

People like Benjamin Franklin are said, for this reason, to have 'incomplete records'. This means simply that a full double entry system of bookkeeping is not maintained.

Recording almost everything and more

Given that many small businesses do not operate a full double entry system, how can they best satisfy the requirements of the Inland Revenue? And for the business's own purposes of control, what is the best policy? The answer is that to satisfy both demands, you need to keep records that will enable you to produce an accurate set of accounts. Keeping an analysed cash book, which is balanced each month, and supported by bank statements, invoices, paying-in books and cheque book stubs, should allow you to do this.

If you are not a limited company, or a VAT registered company, the minimum records you would be advised to keep comprise:

- *A cash book*
  This records all your cash income and expenses, and all your bank receipts and payments.
- *Petty cash book*
  This records small day-to-day cash expenses and the cash drawn from the bank to meet them.
- *A full record of your income*
  This could be a daily record of takings, copies of all sales invoices, details of any other cash receipts and bankings.
- *Purchase invoices*
  These support all your purchases for the business.
- *Copies of loan, HP or other financing agreements*
  You may have used these to purchase assets for the business or provide money for working capital.
- *Bank records*
  Bank statements, cheque book stubs, paying-in books.

- *Debtors and creditors*
  List of amounts owing to your business and amounts owed by your business.
- *Stock and work in progress*
  These should be valued at least once a year, usually at your accounting year end.
- *Cash in hand*
  This should be counted as you go through the year, and compared with the theoretical balance in your cash book.

Pitfalls

These records constitute the minimum necessary to produce accurate accounts. Keeping these records provides a good basic framework for accuracy and control. But you may, for your own reasons, be happy keeping more records than these.

If you fail to keep the minimum records required, you may face penalties. Should a business be investigated in depth by the Inland Revenue, and its records be found to be inadequate, attempts to reconstruct its pattern of income will be made using various detective-style techniques. Diary, appointments books, job estimates and business correspondence may be examined in order to provide figures. Ultimately, an estimate may be made. For the taxpayer, the process can be a nightmare. Good records can help to avoid this happening.

Keeping good records has the following advantages:

- More accurate accounts
- Simpler tax affairs
- Risk of penalties minimised
- Control of business enhanced
- More accurate budgets and forecasts made possible
- Aid to decision making

Recording stock and work in progress

There are some types of information which may not be recorded in your day-to-day records. The most important categories are stock and work in progress. These are key figures which affect your profit.

At the end of any accounting period, you need to take stock. Knowing what your stock-take is aiming to do, you will be able to choose the best method for you.

All retail and manufacturing businesses take stock. Stock in such cases is called stock-in-trade, which is counted and valued at the price it cost the business. Some people use approximations to actual cost: in manufacturing businesses, for example, it may be difficult to work out what the actual cost is. In retailing, stock-in-trade is counted at full selling price, and then an allowance is made on each type of goods for the mark-up percentage used. This is often a fairly accurate estimate of cost price.

Other businesses too have stock. All businesses will have stationery, spares, perhaps fuel at the year end. These items are usually called expense stocks. Sometimes no adjustment is made for these in the accounts but if levels are high, or tend to vary a great deal, it is best to value them. They will affect your profit.

Work in progress is not usually recorded in the books as you go along. It is the value of work on hand at any particular time. At your accounting year end you need to consider the level of work in progress if you are going to get an accurate profit figure. Work in progress is not stock. Work in progress represents the value of goods or work done, materials supplied for a particular customer, which have not actually been billed to that person.

Keeping records of non-business income

Keeping records of income received in your private life can be useful too. There are a number of reasons why you might want to keep track of non-business income.

- To record investment income (see Chapter 7)
- If you make a capital gain (see Chapter 7)
- If you are in business and the Inland Revenue asks in-depth questions

Inland Revenue in-depth investigations

If you are in business, there is always the chance that the Inland Revenue will subject your affairs to an in-depth investigation. (The procedure is described in more detail in Chapter 2.) If this happens, you are likely to be asked to explain where money received in your private accounts has come from. Should you be unable to provide proof of such sources of income, you run the risk that the Revenue will treat unidentified receipts as undeclared business income. This is particularly the case if your business records are poor. It is therefore wise to keep full documentation for non-business receipts, especially for large sums, such as legacies, gifts or prize money of any kind.

A guide to cash books

The cash book – why and how?

The central core of the accounting records of a business should be its cash book. The purpose of a cash book is not just to record what has happened in the past, but to enable you to manage what will happen in the future. It should allow you to manage your bank balance and help you to identify any discrepancies in cash. If you write up your cash book in arrears from your bank statements and cash vouchers, it will provide only a record of what has happened. If you write it up as you go along, every day or every week, as you process your receipts and payments, it becomes a tool to help you manage your bank and cash accounts. This procedure puts you in the driving seat, controlling what is going to happen.

What sort of cash book?

For many businesses, a ruled bound book will be suitable. It may still be appropriate even if other records, such as sales records, are kept on computer. The main decisions you need to think about relate to the number of columns you are going to analyse the figures into, and what categories of expenses you are going to use.

How many columns? Think about:

- The size and complexity of your business
- Whether you keep any other records, eg sales and purchase ledgers
- The importance of cash transactions in your business
- Whether you are registered for VAT
- Whether you are on a VAT retail scheme

Typical expense heading and groupings:

- Purchases
- Rent, rates and insurance
- Heat and light
- Motor
- Repairs and renewals
- Printing, postage and stationery
- Telephone
- Advertising
- Sundries
- Miscellaneous

There are many pre-printed cash books on the market. Some are designed for specific types of business, such as shops. They provide a ready-made framework for analysing your expenses and for balancing and summarising your figures. If you are thinking of asking a firm of accountants to prepare your year-end figures, however, you would be well advised to check with them first, in case they require a specific layout.

See Figures 5.1, 5.2 and 5.3.

You can lay your cash book out to suit the needs of your business. The example in Figure 5.1 shows some simple expense and receipts headings and how to use them. The basic lay-out records only bank receipts and payments. It could be adapted to cope with more complicated circumstances (see Figure 5.3).

Receipts for the month of June 1994

Date	Customer/Description	Invoice no	Sales & work done	Own monies invested	Other receipts	Total banked
June 1	R Stone	171	450 —			450 —
1	Insurance refund	see letter			65 —	65 —
8	E Franklin	153	650 45			650 45
10	Loan to business account	B/S a/c		1000 00		1000 00

Figure 5.1 *Cash book lay-out*

Expenses for the month of June 1994

Date	Supplier/Description	Receipt no.	Purchases	Motor expenses	Telephone postage & stationery	Rent rates & insurances	Heat & light	Sundries/repairs	Private expenses	Total bank
June 8	Rosco Ltd stock	389	455 72							455 72
8	S Power electricity	390					188 17			188 17
8	Hassans garage petrol a/c	391		97 59						97 59
5	Transfer to private a/c								900 00	900 00
5	B Telecom telephone a/c	392			186 13					186 13
5	B Telecom new acess m/c	393						137 95		137 95
12	Deposit on new machine	394						1000 00		1000 00

Figure 5.1 *continued*

Receipts for the week ending 11th June 1994

Date	Takings	Standard rated sales	Zero rated sales	Total receipts					
	Sunday								
	Monday								
	Tuesday								
	Wednesday								
	Thursday								
	Friday								
	Saturday								
	Sales exempt from VAT								
	Total takings								
	Other receipts								
	Cash from bank								
	Cash refunds								
	Refunds of VAT								
	Own money introduced								
	Sales of equipment								
	Cash in hand at start								
	of week								
	Total for balancing cash		£						

Figure 5.2 *Weekly income record for cash-based businesses*

Expenses for the month of June 1993

Date	Description	Ref no	Business expenses	Private expenses	Cash to bank	VAT	Total cash	Total bank
June 8	Telephone telephone a/c	153	145 12			25 40		170 52
8	Banking				1350 —		1350 —	
4	Stamps	134	5 40				5 40	
5	Wages for staff		110 00				110 00	

Figure 5.3 *Coping with cash and VAT*

If your income is mainly in cash you will need to record your daily takings. This is usually the case in retail businesses. The lay-out in Figure 5.2 is a good starting point.

If you are registered for VAT, you may be able to use the standard rated sales and zero rated sales columns. Your output tax for the week is then 7/47 of the standard rated sales. Some businesses, especially retail businesses operating a retail scheme, may need separate workings instead.

If you are not registered for VAT, simply ignore the references to it.

Note that business expenses in Figure 5.3 have been grouped together for simplicity. In practice you need to analyse them into different expense headings, as illustrated in the text and in Figure 5.1.

This lay-out shows the additional complications of VAT registration and recording cash payments.

If you are on the cash accounting scheme for VAT, you can isolate the VAT you pay in your cash book. Your business expenses are then shown net of VAT.

If you are not on the cash scheme, you would normally recover VAT from your invoices. This may be done in your purchase records or by using a separate VAT book.

What to do with your purchase invoices

Purchase invoices are the bills you pay when you buy something. When you buy goods or services, you can end up with a variety of documents, ranging from simple till receipts to delivery notes, invoices and statements. You may also receive a receipt for payment in due course. Of all these papers, the invoice is the one you most need to keep and file. For most small businesses, a ring binder is one of the best ways to keep your purchase invoices under control.

- *Till receipts*
  If you have only a till receipt, mark on it what it was for, and treat it as an invoice.

- *Delivery notes*
  If you have delivery notes, check them against the invoice when it arrives and file the two together.
- *Statements*
  If you pay to statement, it may be appropriate to file the invoices together with the statement. Always keep the invoice!

The best way of organising your file of purchase invoices depends on how you run the business. The fundamental question is whether you account on a cash basis for your purchases or on a credit basis.

Cash basis

- You enter and analyse purchases you make in your cash book when you pay for them.
- The main record you use is a cash book.
- If you are registered for VAT, you are on the cash accounting scheme.

If this is how you operate, the best way to treat your purchase invoices is as follows:

- Put your unpaid purchase invoices in a file with a summary total at the front. This summary lists the total amounts owing to your suppliers. The purchase invoices can be filed either in date order or grouped by supplier.
- File your paid invoices in the same order as you write the payments out in your cash book. You can cross-reference them by giving each a number.

The numbers should run in a completely unbroken series and there should be no duplication.

Credit basis

- You enter and analyse your purchases when you receive an invoice.
- You may use a purchase day book, or a purchases account, linked with a purchase ledger.

- No adjustments are made to the analysis when payment is made. Payments are simply analysed in the cash book as 'purchase ledger'.
- If you are registered for VAT, you account for VAT on the basis of movement of goods and supply of documentation rather than on the basis of payment date.

If this is how you operate, it will be best to file your purchase invoices in the same order as your day book or purchase ledger account. Give each invoice a unique reference number. Statements can be filed separately once they have been checked. Delivery notes can be filed with invoices.

What to do with your sales invoices

Sales invoices record your income: they are the bills you send out. The position here is similar to that of payments, but there is one large difference. The paperwork starts with you. The essential thing is for you to keep copies of all the sales invoices you send out. Obviously in a cash-based retail business, this is impracticable. Here you need to rely on till rolls and a daily cash count to record your daily takings accurately.

File all your sales invoices together – again, a ring binder is adequate for many small businesses. The main feature of your file of sales invoices should be that it is a *complete* record of your sales, and that it is obvious to any third party that it is complete. You can do this by giving each invoice a reference number of its own, with the reference numbers running in an unbroken series. When your invoices are paid, file them according to the series number, even if payment is received in a different order from this. Numbering and presenting your sales invoices in this way is a good defence against any suggestion — for example, by the Revenue – that there are sales which have not been declared.

If you send out reminders when people are slow in paying, make sure that reminders cannot in any way be confused with your bills. It is best if they are in a completely different form from your bills. This helps to avoid confusion. If you use a duplicate invoice book for your bills, don't use the next page for a reminder or statement; use a separate book. This way your duplicate book remains a full record of your sales without entries doubled up or confusing cross references.

Coping with credit sales can be relatively straightforward. If you don't have such a large volume of customers that you can justify keeping a sales ledger or computerised sales system, try the following method:

Unpaid sales invoices
- File unpaid copy sales invoices in numerical order. Keep a list of unpaid bills and the grand total at the front of this file.

On payment of sales invoices
- When you receive payment, mark the date of payment on the copy sales invoice.
- Enter the sales reference number against the receipt in your cash book.
- Change the grand total on the list at the front of the file of unpaid copy sales invoices.
- Mark the date of payment on this list.
- Transfer the copy of the invoice which has been paid to your separate paid invoice file.
- File paid invoices in numerical order. This means that when all bills have been paid, the numerical sequence in the file of paid invoices will be complete. When some are outstanding, there will be gaps in the sequence, but the missing copy bills will be in the unpaid file, and included as unpaid in the listing at the front.

Using a computer

Computers are designed to work in real time. They will update your position with a posting routine in minutes. To manage computer records, you need to decide when and how often to take hard copy. A computer may not keep any records of the past. It may be unable to produce the previous version of a file that you have just updated. In these circumstances, if you need a version of that file for reference, you will have to make sure that procedures and routines are set up so that material is processed in the right order, and that timely copies are made.

In many businesses, record keeping is only partially computerised. There may be a computerised sales and purchase system but a manual cash book. Your system may not be integrated. If this is the case, check that you have control totals to ensure that the various computerised and manual records have all reached the same point at the same time. You do not want the cash book to show that a payment has been made or received when the sales or purchase ledger shows that the transaction is still pending.

The best guide to choosing a computer package is practice. It is almost impossible to envisage in advance all the things you may want it to do. The system may provide impressive banks of information, but be inflexible in one particular that you find useful – so useful you don't consider it possible for the machine to be unable to cope. If you can find someone who has a system similar to the one you are contemplating and familiarise yourself with it, this will be your best course of action. Above all, don't feel that you have to be computerised. There are costs, learning curves and new problems to encounter. Perhaps you should start with a manual system to see what sort of records you find most useful before choosing a computer system.

How long to keep records

- For income tax purposes
  Usually six years
- For limited companies
  Three years for a private company
  Six years for a public company
- VAT records
  Six years
- PAYE wages records
  Three years after the end of the year they concern

---

6. Preparing figures

The annual accounts prepared for most self-employed people show what business profits are being made. The profit is then adjusted for income tax purposes, so that the Revenue receives your accounts plus a set of income tax computations.

Annual accounts prepared for you may include expenses of a business nature which are not allowable for tax purposes. These are the sorts of item which require adjustment in the tax computations – see Figure 6.1.

The key to understanding your annual accounts and getting the most out of them is outlined in the first half of the chapter.

If you want to prepare figures for yourself, you can instead prepare one set of figures calculated solely to show your tax liability. If you do this, you should include in your figures all sources of taxable income, and only expenses which are allowable for tax purposes. Guidance on how to do this is given in the second part of this chapter.

Understanding your accounts – checklist of key concepts

- *Accruals*
  Amounts owed by you which you may not yet have been billed for. For example, electricity used since your last bill.
- *Balance sheet*
  List of assets and liabilities of a business, showing what you own and how it is funded.
- *Capital account*
  Your stake in the business.

Mr T. Brown   Ref.123.45678

Income Tax and Capital Allowances Computation

Accounts for the Year Ended 31 December 1993

Adjustment of profit				£
Profit per accounts				26,808
Add: Depreciation				2,997
Private proportions –	Private motoring 1,933 × 80%			1,546
	Private telephone 342 × 30%			103
	Private heating and lighting 810 × 35%			284
Entertaining expenses				110
Less: Bank interest received				(124)
Schedule D Case 1 Profit				31,724

Assessments

1994–95

Adjusted profit			31,724
Capital allowances			1,622
Net assessment			30,102

Capital allowances

	Motor vehicle Bentley	*Private use 80%*	*Pool*	*Claim*
1994–95				
Brought forward	7,500		4,988	
Writing down allowance	1,875	(1,500)	1,247	1,622
Carried forward	5,625		3,741	
Claim				1,622

Note: 'Pool' includes the cost of all equipment and machinery (none used privately) used in the business.

Figure 6.1 *Computation of profit as adjusted for income tax purposes*

The normal procedure is to send a set of financial accounts to the Revenue each year, accompanied by a computation of profit adjusted for income tax purposes. Typical adjustments include depreciation, private use of business assets and a claim for capital allowances. These are shown above.

- *Creditors*
  Amounts owed by your business. For example, for purchase of goods or equipment.
- *Current assets*
  Stocks of goods, work in progress and debts due to the business which are likely to be turned into money within 12 months. Also cash at the bank and cash in hand.
- *Current liabilities*
  Sums your business owes that are likely to be paid within the next 12 months. These include overdrafts, short-term loans, current HP instalments, trading debts.
- *Debtors*
  Amounts owed to your business. For example, for sales of goods.
- *Depreciation*
  An allowance for wear and tear or loss in value of vehicles and equipment used in your business.
- *Drawings*
  Amounts that you take out of the business for your own use.
- *Fixed assets*
  Items you have bought which will be used for a number of years in your business.
- *Gross profit*
  Profit you have made on the sale and purchase of goods before deducting overheads.
- *HP creditor*
  Capital amount owed to an HP company.
- *Intangible fixed assets*
  Items like goodwill or patent rights that you pay for for the long-term benefit of your business.
- *Net profit*
  Profit made after deducting all business costs.
- *Prepayments*
  Things you have paid for in advance, the entire benefits of which you have not yet had.
- *Profit and loss account*
  Summary of your income and your overheads for a specified period.

BENJAMIN FRANKLIN   CANDLE MAKER

TRADING AND PROFIT AND LOSS ACCOUNT
FOR THE YEAR ENDED 30 JUNE 1994

	1994	
	£	£
Sales		179,635
COST OF SALES		
Opening stock	6,364	
Purchases of materials	66,741	
	73,105	
Closing stock	7,735	
		(65,370)
GROSS PROFIT		114,265
LESS OVERHEADS		
Motor expenses	3,953	
Wages	49,537	
Rent and rates	12,563	
Insurance	1,489	
Repairs and renewals	4,186	
Heating, lighting and power	6,112	
Telephone charges	1,480	
Advertising	2,082	
Printing, postage and stationery	108	
Sundry expenses	86	
Bank charges	959	
Bank interest	2,568	
Bank loan interest	899	
Accountancy charges	845	
Depreciation	2,815	
		(89,682)
NET PROFIT FOR THE YEAR		£24,583

Note: For simplicity these figures have not been presented as a manufacturing account.

Figure 6.2 *Example of a trading and profit and loss account*

- *Tangible fixed assets*
  Physical items of equipment, vehicles, land and buildings used in your business.
- *Taxable profit*
  Profit you will be taxed on. This usually differs from the net profit shown on your accounts.

BENJAMIN FRANKLIN CANDLE MAKER
BALANCE SHEET AS AT 30 JUNE 1994

	1994	
	£	£
FIXED ASSETS		8,445
CURRENT ASSETS		
Stock	7,735	
Work in progress	3,762	
Trade debtors	18,101	
Prepayments	1,140	
Cash in hand	1,756	
	32,494	
CURRENT LIABILITIES		
Bank loan	4,034	
Trade creditors	4,284	
Accruals	2,436	
VAT account	6,212	
Bank overdraft	11,362	
	28,328	
NET CURRENT ASSETS		4,166
		£12,611
REPRESENTED BY:		
CAPITAL ACCOUNT		
Opening capital		16,668
Net profit for year		24,583
		41,251
Drawings	17,641	
Tax paid	7,731	
Pensions contributions	3,268	
		(28,640)
TOTAL ASSETS LESS TOTAL LIABILIITIES		£12,611

Figure 6.3 *Example of a balance sheet*

- *Trading account*
  Financial summary used for businesses that buy and sell goods.
  It shows your total income from the sale of goods and the cost
  of purchasing the goods adjusted for changes in stock. It is
  usually combined with a profit and loss account.

What are the figures supposed to show?

Your annual accounts show how your business is performing.

The figures will normally be presented as a profit and loss account and a balance sheet. Examples are given in Figures 6.2 and 6.3. Accounts like these provide information for making decisions. Is enough money being made to cover replacement of assets and cover costs? This is the type of question which can be decided with the help of your accounts.

Your annual accounts, if prepared by a qualified accountant, are likely to be prepared with an eye to certain concepts:

- Accruals or matching basis
- Going concern basis
- Treading with care
- Standard accounting practice

Accruals or matching basis

When you are faced with making business decisions, the basis on which you prepare figures plays an important role. With the accruals or matching basis, the aim is to match up income you have earned and the expenses involved in earning that income. This is irrespective of when you actually received the income or paid for the expenses. The alternative would be to use a cash basis. On a cash basis, income, expenses and profit would reflect the actual movement of money.

If you wanted some figures to help you to decide whether a particular area of your business is profitable, you could come up with one answer if you use figures prepared on a cash basis and another answer if figures are prepared on an accruals basis. Most people would agree that, where the two bases produce different results, the accruals or matching basis is far more important in decision making.

Going concern basis

The going concern basis is also used in preparing figures. Basically, it assumes that a business has a future. If trade ceases, the business may not get refunds of any money paid in advance. It may not be able to collect all the money due in: equipment may have little value second-hand, and there may be additional costs such as redundancy payments. This again would produce a different set of figures.

Treading with care

Common sense is fundamental to accounts. In technical language it is referred to as the 'concept of prudence'. Broadly speaking, it means that if there is significant doubt whether a source of income is likely to materialise, or if there is some possibility of a loss, the doubtful income is excluded, and the likely costs are included.

Standard accounting practice

There are always uncertainties in business. In drawing up accounts, certain decisions have to be made about these issues. How long is a particular piece of machinery going to last? How should the interest on a finance agreement be allocated? What value should be put on goodwill? There are guidelines for these things. 'Statements of Standard Accounting Practice', agreed by the main professional accountancy bodies, give guidance and prescribe treatment in contentious areas. They aim at the production of figures which provide a good basis for making comparisons, and which are consistent.

Figures and reality

Now you have your figures. What do you make of them? The key to understanding your accounts and getting the most out of them is to bridge the gap between how it feels to be in business and what the figures say.

How it feels to be in business is likely to be determined by:

- *Volume of work*
  The volume of work you have to do, and the number of hours you put in.
- *Cash flow*
  How easy you find it to pay your suppliers on time and whether people pay you on time.
- *Financial flexibility*
  Whether there are certain times of year when you find that you need more credit: whether you have difficulties obtaining money to acquire new equipment and vehicles.

- *Expansion*
  Whether you feel your business is expanding.
- *Drawings*
  How much money you take out of the business, and whether you can maintain this level or increase it.

Your accounts will give you information about these factors, but only if you make the right comparisons. You may need to do some arithmetic of your own. The figures you come up with can put you in control.

Volume of work

The volume of work you do is shown as the turnover or total sales figure. Remember that this may have been adjusted for amounts that are due to you but have not yet been paid at the accounting year end, or even at the previous year end. It may also have been adjusted for work in progress, discounts that you have given, and bad debts.

If your work involves charging an hourly rate, the following calculation may come up with interesting results. Divide the total sales figure by your hourly rate. Use an average if necessary. The result is the number of hours' income you have earned. The figure may surprise you. Work out how many hours per week, excluding holidays, that this figure represents. If this is close to the number of hours you put in, you are not losing uncharged time. If it is significantly less, there must be uncharged hours. Try recording all your hours for a week and see what happens.

Benjamin Franklin is a design consultant and usually charges £26.50 per hour. Turnover for the year to 30 April 1994 is £34,435. This is equivalent to 34,435 ÷ 26.5 = 1299 hours charged.

Assuming that there are 46 working weeks in a year, this is equivalent to 28 hours a week charged. If Benjamin Franklin actually works on average 35 hours per week, the extra seven hours a week must represent uncharged time. This might have been eaten up in general administrative work, preliminary work on jobs that are not continued, or it might quite simply represent unrecorded hours spent on chargeable jobs.

The business question that arises is how Benjamin Franklin feels about the pattern of chargeable time. Does he feel that this result is acceptable?

The actual hourly rate that he is getting is $34,435 \div 35$ hours $\div$ 46 weeks = £21.39. With this information to hand, does he want to make an addition to his overall charge-out rate in order to account for administrative time and abortive contracts? Alternatively, he could set up a new time recording system which would highlight the hours not being charged.

A similar procedure can be used to verify your turnover if you use a particular mark-up. See if the actual results show a similar margin, and investigate the possibility that wastage and other losses are changing the margins. Where time and materials are included, exclude the materials from sales first, and then check the labour rates.

Cash flow

Cash flow is not directly shown in accounts but you can use them to look for trends. Compare the current year's accounts and the previous year's, and look on the balance sheet at the figure for debtors. If the debtors' figure has increased, can you think of a good explanation, or is it an area that needs your attention? How have your cash and bank balances changed over the two years? Is the level of trade credit increasing or decreasing? Is it moving in the same direction as debtors? If they are moving in opposite directions, you may well be feeling squeezed.

Financial flexibility

Financial flexibility is also shown on the balance sheet. There are two lines to look at here. The first is net current assets/net current liabilities. The second is the total at the bottom of the column: total assets less total liabilities.

In general, the larger the figure for net current assets, the greater your financial flexibility. However, it also pays to look at the figure for loans: often these are included as current liabilities but they may not be repayable for a number of years.

Expansion

How do you know if your business is expanding? To find out, you can compare the total sales from year to year, as well as the net profit. Keep in mind also the business's level of borrowing and the degree of assets you have backing the business.

Drawings

How much should you take out of the business? The accounts will give you some guidance here. When the figures were prepared, some provision will have been made for replacement of business assets, and their cost will have been spread to reflect the period over which they are likely to benefit the business. However, for sole traders and partnerships, provision is not made for income tax and National Insurance before the profit figure is arrived at. Neither is the cash position apparent from the profit figure. This means that you cannot use the profit figure on the accounts as a guide to how much money you can take out of the business without making some adjustments.

There is a useful pointer to watch:

* *Capital account*
  – On the balance sheet for a sole trader or partnership, there is a capital account. This represents your stake in the business.
  – If the capital account is increasing, or remains stable, the level of money you take out of the business is sensible.
  – If the capital account is a negative figure, it is overdrawn. If this is so, you are taking out more than the business can support.
  – If the balance on the capital account is decreasing, unless you expect profits to increase next year, you are taking out too much.

If your profits vary much from year to year, it may be more difficult to decide on a sensible level of drawings. Tips to remember here are that accounts profits give a view of the medium term. They represent what has happened, not necessarily what is going to happen next. And fundamentally, a business needs cash to survive – even if it makes high profits. A profitable business can fail through lack of cash.

Preparing figures for the inland revenue

What income should you include?

If you want to prepare figures for the Revenue yourself, you can do so. The following guidance is relevant to businesses run by one or more self-employed people – sole traders or partners.

What income should you include? The easiest way to answer this is simply to say that you should include every kind of income, except those you are specifically allowed to leave out! This means that in go rebates and allowances, casual fees and tips, goods you have taken out of the business for your own use. But you can leave out:

- *Bank interest received on a business account*
  This will usually have been taxed at source. But even if it is paid gross, it should not be included in your business profits: it should be disclosed separately on your income tax return.

- *Rental income received*
  Rental income should be disclosed separately on the tax return. However, if it is incidental to your trade (for example, if you sub-let part of your business premises) it can be included as business income.

- *Capital sums from sale of assets*
  Capital sums received from the sale of business or private assets, are treated separately.

- *Loans*
  If you have borrowed money from a lending institution, or privately from family or friends, do not include the receipt as business income.

- *Private money paid into the business*
  It is best to state that you have paid money into the business, and give the source of such money, even though it is not treated as business income.

- *Compensation payments*
  Compensation payments for personal accidents and some other compensation receipts need not be included.

- *Tax refunds*
  If you receive a tax refund, with or without interest (repayment supplement), this need not be included.

- *VAT*
  VAT registered traders do not include VAT in the figures. Usually accounts are prepared excluding VAT as well as any receipts or payments from Customs and Excise. Check that VAT is excluded properly. The VAT account should cancel out, leaving no effect on your trading figures.
- *Grants*
  Grants, especially for capital items, may need to be excluded.
- *Business start-up allowance*
  This is not included as part of your business income but declared separately on your income tax return.

A special case: trading income taxed at source

If you receive trading income taxed at source, it is important to remember that you must state the gross amount as income, not the amount after tax. This is especially relevant for sub-contractors in the construction industry, many of whom work on the SC60 scheme. Here 25 per cent tax is deducted by the main contractor and a certificate stating that this has been done passed to the sub-contractor. Credit for the tax that has been paid is given when the certificate is sent to the Inland Revenue.

What expenses are deductible?

Since all income is included as business income unless there is a specific case for leaving it out, it will come as no surprise that the Inland Revenue's rules on expenses are that they are all to be left out unless there is a good reason for putting them in!

When you are self-employed, there is one general rule to bear in mind when deciding whether you can claim an expense. It is that the expense must be money which is wholly and exclusively laid out or expended for the purpose of your trade, profession or vocation. There are a number of back-up rules which specify other items which cannot be deducted. These include:

- Equipment and machinery
- Domestic expenses
- Rent for domestic accommodation
- Any capital used in the business

- Any allowance for interest you have lost by using money in the business
- Any insured losses
- The cost of purchasing land and buildings

Separate rules apply to many of these categories, such as equipment and machinery, and these are described below.

The steps to use to check if an expense can be deducted are as follows:

- One purpose or two?
- Was it actually spent?
- Did it help the earning capacity of the business?

One purpose or two?

Decide if the expense serves just one purpose: is it entirely and only for business use? This is the 'wholly and exclusively' test.

If the expense is wholly and exclusively for the purpose of your business, you are on the right track.

Work out whether your expense serves a dual purpose. Any item where there is a dual purpose is not allowed. Examples of dual purpose include clothing and food. These are not usually allowed. The law takes the line that you would have fed and clothed yourself whether or not you were in business! Clothing with a safety function may be allowable. If you were a medieval knight a suit of armour would probably pass the test. Meals taken as part of a conference or course related to your work may also be allowable.

Dual purpose also occurs if you work from home. Your heat and light, and other such costs, will all have two purposes: they will be used in your private life as well as for the business. The tactic that is usually adopted here is to split the total cost of such expenses, and allocate some to the business and some to private use. A general claim for the use of home as office can be based on a fraction; for example, the number of rooms that you actually use for a business purpose, divided by the total number of rooms in the house. It is important to remember, however, that if you

use one room at home *only* as an office, you may become liable
to capital gains tax when you sell the house. For this reason, many
people who work from home often use a room as an office *and* a
spare bedroom. In this way the room is not used only for business
purposes.

Motor expenses may also fit into the dual purpose category. Here
the Revenue will frequently accept a certain percentage of your
motor costs as deductible expenses. Again, this is likely to be a
percentage of the total costs; perhaps 50 or 60 per cent, depending on how much business mileage you do in a year. To work out
what is a reasonable percentage split, it may help to record
exactly what mileage you do for business purposes, and how
much for private purposes, for a short while – say, a month or so
each year. It would be possible then to split all your motor costs,
not just fuel, on this basis.

Was it actually spent?

To be deductible, you must actually have spent money on a certain item. It cannot just be an allowance or an estimate, or a
provision to compensate you for what you would have done with
the money if you hadn't used it in the business.

Did it help the earning capacity of the business?

The rules state that the expense must have been made for the
purpose of the business. In other words, it must be involved in
the earning capacity of the business. The item need not, strictly
speaking, be necessary – you may not need a 1922 Bentley to
drive round your farm, for example – but it has to have a purpose
in your business.

There are a number of areas where you have to tread carefully.
Two good examples are interest that you pay and repairs.

Interest

Tax relief on interest that you pay is not automatic for people
who are self-employed. There are two guidelines:

- Was the money borrowed exclusively:
  - for trading purposes?
  - to finance purchase of business equipment?
  - to buy a stake in a business?
- Is there any private benefit?
  Private benefits include the position where the money you have taken out of the business is greater than your profits and cash investment in the business.

If the money is borrowed exclusively for the business, the interest should be allowable. If there is an element of private benefit, there may be a restriction on interest relief. Not all interest relief is given in the same way. Usually it is treated as a trading expense, but some – for example, that used to buy a stake in a partnership business – may be treated as a deduction from your total income.

Repairs

The position with regard to repairs can be complex: one set of rules governs the purchase of *new* equipment and buildings, and another set govern the repair of existing equipment and buildings. If the repairs are extensive, it may seem that what you have created is in effect a new asset. This could mean that you would not be allowed to deduct the expense *in total* from your income for the current year.

This does not mean that you will not get tax relief: it may simply be a question of timing, which affects when you get relief. Essentially only running expenses may be deducted in their entirety from the current year's profits. Expenses of a longer-term nature are covered by separate rules. The prime examples of long-term expenses are equipment and buildings.

Buying equipment and buildings

Equipment and buildings are long-term assets. Getting tax relief here involves a different procedure. Tax relief is given for long-term business assets which fall into certain specified categories. These include:

- Machinery and plant – including vehicles
- Industrial buildings used for manufacturing

- Agricultural and forestry buildings and improvements
- Hotels
- Dredging
- Toll roads
- Expenditure on know-how
- Mines and oil wells
- Patent rights
- Scientific research

Each group has its own detailed rules and rates of relief. Some modifications apply for particular industries, such as film companies, and for some areas, such as enterprise zones.

Unless you are an oil baron with a chain of hotels, a handful of dredgers, a couple of toll roads, pine forests, a landed estate or two, and a keen interest in Newtonian physics, the two categories most likely to be relevant to you are plant and machinery, and industrial buildings.

Industrial buildings

Relief is given for expenditure on qualifying new industrial buildings, or industrial buildings under 25 years old, at the rate of 4 per cent of cost for each year they are in use.

Plant and equipment

The basic allowance given for plant and equipment is 25 per cent of the balance of the cost each year. Such allowances are known as capital allowances. The November 1993 Budget introduced a time limit for the claiming of capital allowances. For self-employed people these claims will have to be made within 12 months of the date the accounts are due to be filed.

Working out a claim

Benjamin Franklin, self-employed candle maker and song writer, buys a printer for his computer. It costs £1200. It is to be used exclusively for the business.

Year 1 of claim
Maximum claim of £1200 × 25% = £300

Year 2 of claim
The sum represents 25% of the balance of the cost:
claim of 25% × (1200 − £300) (the amount you claimed last year)
= £225

The calculation is not always this straightforward. There are a number of special circumstances:

- First year in business
- Year of claim
- Selling equipment
- Using assets privately
- When to claim
- Increased rate of claim

First year in business

If it is your first year in business, you have to scale the claim down. The maximum claim is 25 per cent multiplied by the number of days you were trading in the first tax year. This is divided by 365, the number of days in a year.

Year of claim

Claims are made for tax years, not for accounting years. In other words, claims run from 6 April in one year to 5 April in the next. Until sweeping changes in procedure are implemented in 1996, this means that in the early years of a business, the amount you can claim may not be related to your current set of accounts.

Selling equipment

If you sell a piece of equipment, an adjustment is made. Assets with private use (including motor cars) are usually treated separately. If you sell these, you will either be given more allowances or taxed if a profit is made. Other assets are usually grouped together. If you sell any of these items, the sale proceeds are taken away from the value of the group. Usually this means that your claim for capital allowances, in the year you make a sale, is a little reduced. Sometimes there may be additional tax to pay.

Using assets privately

If you use any asset for private purposes, the amount of the claim has to be reduced proportionately.

Benjamin Franklin has just purchased a car. It cost £10,000 and is used mostly for business. Business use is 60 per cent, private use 40 per cent. The maximum claim for capital allowances in the year of purchase would be:

$$£10,000 \times 25\% \times 60\% = £1500$$

However, the claim next year will be calculated as if Benjamin Franklin had claimed the full 25 per cent allowance in the first year. The maximum claim in the second year is therefore:

$$£7,500 \times 25\% \times 60\% = £1125$$

The way this works can be shown in figure 6.4.

Year of purchase	*Motor car*	*Claim*
Cost of car	10,000	
Maximum claim @ 25% × 10,000	2,500	2,500
Restriction on claim for private use 40% × 2500	–	(1,000)
Maximum claim in first year (2500 × 60%)	‾‾‾‾	1,500
Balance of expenditure carried forward to next year (10,000 – 2500)	7,500	
Second year claim		
7500 × 25% maximum	1,875	1,875
Private use restriction @ 40%		(750)
Maximum claim in second year (1,875 × 60%)		1,125
Balance carried forward to next year	£5,625	

Figure 6.4 *Your claim with private use*

When to claim

You do not have to make a claim in every year. It may, in fact, be to your advantage not to make a claim. This may happen if your income is low. It is also possible to make a partial or a restricted claim rather than a full, usually a 25 per cent, claim. If you make a restricted claim in one year, the size of your claim the next year may be increased. This can be a useful planning point, for example, if you know that you are likely to be taxed at a higher rate in the following year.

Increased rate of claim

For expenditure made between 1 November 1992 and 31 October 1993, a first year claim of 40 per cent was possible. This did not extend to private cars.

Who works out your claim?

You can, if you wish, pass the responsibility for calculating a claim to the Inland Revenue. They will always be prepared to work out a claim for you. It is important to know what information to provide. Always keep a note of the date when you acquire an asset, what the asset is, and what category you think it falls into.

'Simple' tax accounts

In recent years, businesses run by sole traders or partnerships whose annual turnover is below a certain threshold have been allowed to send what are known as 'simple' tax accounts to the Inland Revenue. The turnover threshold is at present £15,000. Figures may be submitted as a three-line summary, showing total turnover, less business expenses, to arrive at a net profit figure. Inland Revenue form 41K, which is included in the leaflet IR 104 'Simple tax accounts', can be used for this purpose.

However, to arrive at your figures, you will still need to apply the tests about what income is to be included, and what expenses may be deducted, described earlier. It is open to the Revenue to ask you to provide information to back up the figures you prepare and, in respects other than the presentation of your figures, normal Revenue procedures and requirements apply. Figures 6.5 and 6.6 show one set of figures presented in two forms: as a profit and loss account and also the 'three-line' format.

R STONE   T/A MEDIEVAL MANUSCRIPTS
TRADING AND PROFIT AND LOSS ACCOUNT
FOR THE YEAR ENDED 31 MARCH 1994

	1994	
	£	£
Sales		8,632
COST OF SALES		
Opening stock	2,395	
Purchases and restoration costs	1,967	
Materials	54	
Commission	120	
	4,536	
Less:		
Closing stock	2,595	
Cost of sales		(1,941)
GROSS PROFIT		6,691
LESS OVERHEADS		
Advertising	103	
Motor expenses	741	
Telephone charges	244	
Printing, postage and stationery	40	
Catalogues and annuals	79	
Heating and lighting	229	
Repairs and renewals	276	
Insurance	503	
Rates	211	
Bank charges	48	
		(2,474)
NET TRADING PROFIT FOR THE YEAR		£4,217

Note: Only business proportions of expenses have been charged.
      No deduction is made for depreciation.

Figure 6.5 *Simple tax accounts: profit and loss account*

Summary of profits from 1 April 1993 to 31 March 1994

To   HMIT Triassic District   Tax Ref. 272 030796

My name is   ROSETTA STONE
The nature of my business is   MEDIEVAL MANUSCRIPT PAINTING
My business address is   WAT TYLER WORKSHOPS
                                    ROYALTY ROAD
                                    WOODTOWN

Turnover   £8,632   Show your total business earnings before
                          expenses

Expenses   £4,415   Show your total business expenses

Profit   £4,217   Take your expenses from your turnover to
                          give your profit

To the best of my knowledge and belief the information I have given
above is correct

Signature   Date:

If you bought or sold any vehicles or machinery which you use in your
business please give details over the page.

∗∗∗

Note: The Revenue will calculate any relief due to you for vehicles and machinery.

Total business expenses are calculated as £1,941 (cost of sales) plus £2,474 (total overheads) equals £4,415.

Figure 6.6 *Presentation of simple tax accounts*

7. Your tax return

Presenting your income and claiming your allowances

Tax returns come in a number of different guises. But whatever the design, the purpose is the same: to record income received and gains made in the previous tax year, and to claim allowances for the year to come. The return includes a declaration that you have to sign stating that the information is true and complete.

Income is recorded under a variety of different headings, such as employment, self-employment, rental income, interest and dividends. Income is split into these categories because different tax rules apply to each.

Do you need a tax return?

Under the Taxes Acts, you, as a taxpayer, have a duty to disclose to the Inland Revenue matters which affect your tax liability. Self-employed people will usually be sent a return automatically and so are provided with the means to make disclosure. Employees are normally taxed at source, and relatively few receive a tax return on a regular basis at present. If an employee's only other income comes from interest from a bank or building society which is taxed, or company dividends, it is unlikely that there will be any outstanding tax liability.

The key to the system, however, is that the emphasis is on you to act: this means that if you acquire a new, and untaxed, source of income, you need to notify the tax office and ask for a tax return. There are penalties for failing to notify the Revenue of your liability to tax. Circumstances which might call for action include:

- Starting self-employment
- Letting out property
- Receiving casual wages
- Receiving interest from a bank or building society which is paid without deduction of tax

But the boot is sometimes on the other foot. There may be circumstances where you think that you are due for a refund of tax, rather than due to pay tax. This would be another good reason for asking the Revenue for an income tax return.

Keeping track of your income

So now you are faced with completing a tax return. It is important that it is complete and accurate. This need not be a daunting task if you keep the right records.

The starting point is to keep a copy of your return each year. If it is not possible to take a photocopy, prepare your own summary or make a note of the figures you put down, perhaps using the Revenue leaflet 'Filling in your tax return', a copy of which you will receive with your return.

It is all too easy to overlook a single dividend receipt, or to forget one instalment of interest received, especially now that many clearing banks add interest to current accounts. The best guide is to lay out your working papers methodically, and keep them to hand to back up the figures you enter on the return. See Figure 7.1. Points to watch are:

Date payable	Payment no.	Company	Holding	Tax credit	Dividend received
2.3.93	41	B Franklin PLC	200	£19.00	£57.00

Lay out a sheet of paper with these headings and insert your figures accordingly. This provides a good framework for your calculations.

Figure 7.1 *Layout for working papers for tax returns*

41 (payment number)   BENJAMIN FRANKLIN   Security code
                             PLC Ordinary shares   0-000-000
                             Interim dividend for year
                             ended 30 June 1993
                             Payable 2 March 1993

                             Tax voucher
                             The attached warrant...

Dr Rosetta Stone
Postcode Mansion
Franklin Street   Secretary: Z Franklin
Someplace
UK

Holding   Tax credit   Dividend payable
200   £19.00   £57.00

Figure 7.2 *Example of dividend voucher*

- *Bank and building society interest*
  - This interest is usually paid on specific dates for each account. Lay out your papers to reflect this and, if you have any gaps, you will notice at once.
  - If you close an account, remember to include the interest received up to the date of closure. It is good policy to write the date of closure on your tax return.
  - Keep track of your capital so you can tell what to expect. If one account has closed, where has the capital gone? Has it been used to open another account?
- *Dividend vouchers*
  - Dividend vouchers usually have consecutive unique serial payment reference numbers. They are usually paid at the same times each year. If you record the payment number, you will be more likely to notice any gaps where vouchers are missing. See Figure 7.2.
  - Remember that for your tax return it is the date of payment that counts, not the year which the payment is in respect of.
- *Capital gains*
  Here you may need records going back a number of years. When you come to sell shares, for example, you need to know the history of your holding. Remember to include not only purchases of shares but scrip and rights issues, subdivision and additional shares received in lieu of dividends.

- *Rental income*
  The tax rules regarding income from rented property vary
  considerably from one type of let to another. More generous
  rules apply to furnished holiday lettings than to other forms of
  let, for example. Unfurnished lets have the least flexibility for
  allowable expenses. Letting losses can only be offset in specific
  ways, depending on the type of lease and sometimes the respec-
  tive responsibilities of landlord and tenant. Lets to family
  members are also treated differently.

To ensure that you can establish the best treatment, therefore, it
is worth recording a few details in addition to expenses and
income. When the property was unlet, the timing of repairs, number of weeks let, and periods that the property was available for
letting, are all useful. If you have a number of properties that are
let, you should record details of income and expenses for each
property separately.

Claiming your allowances

- *Personal allowance*
  Everyone is due a personal allowance. For people over the age
  of 65 there is a higher rate of personal allowance, and for those
  over 75 there is a further increase. Rates in 1994–95 are £3445
  for the under 65s, £4200 for the over 65s, and £4370 for the
  over 75s. The higher rates are, however, subject to income-
  capping.
- *Married couple's allowance*
  The current rate is £1720. Higher rates apply for those over
  65 and 75, the rate here being based on the age of the older
  spouse. The over-65 rate is £2665 and the over-75 rate is
  £2705. From 6 April 1994 these allowances are restricted to
  the 20 per cent band.
    The married couple's allowance is usually given entirely against
  the husband's income, but this can be altered. It is possible now
  to allocate either half to each spouse; the whole to either spouse;
  or to allocate nominally to the husband with the transfer of any
  excess to the wife. However, all these arrangements require you
  to get in touch with the tax office. You will need to make a written
  election to state which allocation you prefer. Some elections must
  be made in advance, before the beginning of the tax year.

- *Widow's bereavement allowance*
  Rate in 1994–95 £1720 (restricted to the 20 per cent band).
- *Additional relief for children*
  Rate in 1994–95 £1720 (restricted to the 20 per cent band).
- *Blind person's allowance*
  Rate in 1994–95 £1200.
- *Flat rate expenses for employees*
  For employees in certain industries, there is a flat rate allowance for the upkeep of tools and special clothing. This ranges from £15 to £125, depending on the industry involved. Alternatively an employee can claim his actual expenses as a deduction. Flat rate allowance is usually given via the PAYE code. To claim the actual expenses, you need a tax return. To see if there is a flat rate agreement for your industry, contact the Revenue. Sectors covered include, for example, agricultural workers, uniformed bank employees, uniformed police officers and prison officers, and railwaymen.
- *Personal pension schemes and retirement annuity payments*
  Tax relief is available here, calculated with reference to your age, your level of earnings and the type of policy.
- *Maintenance payments made under court order for divorcees*
  This is usually restricted to the level of the married couple's allowance. Different rules apply for orders made before 1988.
- *Medical insurance premiums*
  When these are paid under eligible contracts for private medical insurance for UK residents aged 60 or over, basic rate tax relief is given by deduction at source from the payments made. Relief at higher rates, if appropriate, can be claimed on a tax return.
- *Uniform allowances for members of the armed forces*

Timescale for submission

Tax returns are due for submission 30 days from the date of issue. Usually they are issued at the beginning of April, so submission is due in May. However, in practice this timescale is not generally adhered to and, as a working rule, returns should be submitted by 30 September in each year at the latest. If you receive a return that has been re-issued, you have 30 days from the date of re-issue rather than the original timescale.

What happens if your return is late?

If you delay sending in your return, you are likely to be sent a duplicate, often dispatched in the autumn. But there are other points to consider if you delay, apart from receiving a new set of official paperwork through the post.

- *New source of income, or a gain of which the Revenue has previously been unaware?*
  If you are due to disclose such income on your return, and tax is due, you may have to pay interest on the tax. This may happen if the tax is paid late because you have delayed with your tax return.
- *Sub-contractor in the construction industry?*
  Sub-contractors with 714 certificates are required to keep their tax affairs up to date. Sending in regular tax returns is part of this process. If you need to apply for additional 715 vouchers or renew your 714 at a time when your tax return is outstanding, your application is likely to be delayed.
- *Tax relief due?*
  Tax relief due to you, for example, in respect of the married couple's allowance, pension payments or loan interest, may be delayed until your return is submitted.

For these reasons, the best policy is to keep up to date with returns.

When will you be taxed?

Many sources of income are taxed in the tax year that you receive them, for example income from employment, dividend income, taxed bank and building society interest. However, some sources of income are taxed on a different basis. Gross interest received may be taxed on a preceding year basis. The preceding year basis may also apply to self-employed income and income from abroad.

A preceding year basis is often used because it would not normally be possible to know what the correct amount of income is until after the end of the tax year. To tax this income as it arose would involve a certain amount of conjecture.

This, however, is exactly what happens with rental income. Tax on rental income is due on 1 January, and includes income for the period to the 5 April coming. For this purpose it is assumed that the property will continue to be let during this period, and that rates charged will be in line with those already notified to the tax office. These figures may then be revised after the end of the tax year, once a tax return has been submitted.

Taxed in year of receipt

- Income from employment
- Dividend income
- Taxed bank and building society income

Taxed on preceding year basis

- Gross interest
- Income from self-employment (from 6 April 1994 new businesses will be charged on a current year basis)
- Income from abroad

Pitfalls to avoid

- *Tax at source*
  If you have paid tax at source, check what type of tax you have paid, and at what rate. These are the main categories:
  - Basic rate tax deducted
    This means that 25 per cent tax has been withheld from your income as income tax paid on your behalf. It is worth as much to you as if you had paid it yourself. It is refundable in full or in part if appropriate.
  - Tax credits
    These are not payments of income tax on your behalf but may count as such. This is often the position with company dividends. Companies pay corporation tax, and are obliged to pay some in advance whenever they pay a dividend to

shareholders. This is called advance corporation tax. Advance corporation tax paid by the company may be off-set against its own corporation tax bill. But for the person who receives the dividend, it also counts as an income tax credit. In the past, the tax credit for income tax was at basic rate. Since 6 April 1993, the credit is at the lower rate of income tax only, 20 per cent, irrespective of the rate of advance corporation tax paid by the company. If you are due a refund of income tax, the income tax equivalent to the tax credits on dividends can usually be refunded. However, this does not apply when you receive shares in lieu of dividends.

- Notional tax credits
  If you have chosen to receive additional shares in a company rather than a cash dividend, the 'notional tax credit' on these vouchers is not refundable. It can be used only to cover part of your tax liability.

- Investments deemed basic rate paid
  There are also certain investment bonds and other more complicated securities which are deemed basic rate tax paid by virtue of special arrangements between the insurance companies and the Inland Revenue.

• *TESSAs and PEPs*
  Special rules mean that TESSA and PEP accounts are usually tax-exempt. It is possible to break the terms giving tax exemption. If you do so, remember to include the income.

• *State benefits*
  Many State benefits are now taxable. These include unemployment benefit, income support payments made to the unemployed, industrial death benefit, invalid care allowance, invalidity allowance paid with a retirement pension, retirement pension, statutory maternity pay, statutory sick pay and others. Such income is included in your tax return, although the actual figures are usually obtained by the Inland Revenue from the DSS.

• *Benefits in kind*
  Remember to include benefits in kind such as company cars, and any other goods or services provided for your private use by your employer.

- *Other income*

  If you have a source of income but are unsure where to include it on the tax return, enter it in the 'other income' category, or include a separate sheet with your tax return.

- *Changes in circumstances, changes in the rules*

  Watch out for changes in your circumstances and changes in the rules. If you have a home loan under MIRAS, reconsider the position if there are substantial changes. This could happen if, for example, you move into rented accommodation and let out your house. Changes in your residence status may also be important.

- *Keeping papers*

  Try to obtain all the necessary paperwork to support any claims you want to make, either for expenses or for credit for tax paid. These would include:

  - Pensions

    Certificates as evidence of increased premiums or additional policies taken out.

  - Bank or building society interest

    Section 352 certificate of interest paid if you think that you are due a repayment of tax on interest deducted.

  - Loan interest

    MIRAS 5 certificate of loan interest paid to offset against letting income.

- *Calculations*

  Check that your figures seem reasonable. This is the calculation to work out what you receive if you pay 25 per cent basic rate tax on investment income:

The basic rate tax paid (or tax credit) on investment income is one third of the amount you receive. If you receive £75 net income, the tax paid will be £75 ÷ 3 = £25. The gross income will be £75 + 25 = £100.

To work out the gross amount of income when it is basic rate paid, divide the amount you receive by 0.75 (3/4). If you receive £90 net income, the gross amount is £90 ÷ 0.75 = £120.

As a double check, you can multiply the gross amount by the tax rate, and see if the figures make sense: £120 × 25% = £30. £120 gross less £30 tax paid equals £90 net income. For a lower rate tax credit of 20 per cent, use 1/4 and 0.8.

Your repayment claim

The Inland Revenue has now set up special repayment offices to deal with repayment claims. This has been done in part to allow people to recover tax paid at source on investment income. Your nearest repayment office may be outside your area but your local tax office will be able to provide the address.

Filling in the repayment form

The repayment claim form is much simpler than an ordinary tax return. The main points to bear in mind are:

- *Supporting papers*
  You will need to send in your dividend vouchers and certificates of tax paid on interest received, so make sure you obtain them.
- *Include everything!*
  The repayment form is still designed as a full record of your income and allowances, just like a tax return. If you have any doubt about what to include, send a separate sheet with covering notes.
- *Covenants to charity*
  If you make covenants to charity, you are deemed to have paid these after deduction of basic rate tax. This would reduce your refund.

Repayment centres deal relatively swiftly with claims, with the administration kept to a minimum. If you want your papers returned when your claim is processed, mark this clearly on the repayment form.

8. Your tax bill

Assessments – what to check

Tax assessments are sent out by the Inland Revenue. They show you how your tax bill is calculated. It is worth checking the figures in detail to make sure that you are being asked for the correct amount of tax.

Assessments for self-employed sole traders

For people who are self-employed and work as sole traders (not in partnership or through a limited company) the layout of an assessment is like the fictitious assessment for Benjamin Franklin; see Figure 8.1.

Layout : left-hand side

- Top
  - Your tax reference number
  - The tax year
  - The date the assessment was issued
  - Your name and address
  - Your tax office's name and address
  - Paragraph telling you about the assessment
- Bottom
  - Notice to pay

Layout : right-hand side

- Heading states:
  - Your name
  - Assessment number (far right-hand corner)
  - Title – 'Notice of assessment'
  - Tax year
- Income and deductions
- Trading deductions
- Allowances
- Calculation of tax
- Class 4 National Insurance payable

Points to check

Left-hand side
- *The tax year*
  - Is the assessment for the current year or a previous year? If it is a revision of a previous year, are you aware of any reason for the amendment?
  - Knowing what tax year is important because this determines what rates of personal allowances and tax are relevant.
- *Issue date*
  You have 30 days from the date of issue to make any objections to the figures.
- *Name and address*
  Is the assessment properly addressed to you? If you have recently taken over someone else's business, you may be sent, in error, a tax bill payable by your predecessor. If your name is not correctly shown, phone the tax office to inform them of the correct details, and confirm in writing.
- *Paragraph telling you about the assessment*
  This may include a number of details. First, there are standard details:
  - Agent? If you have an agent (eg an accountant), is their name shown? If it is, they will have received a copy and will be able to deal with the assessment for you. If you have signed Inland Revenue authority form 64-8 a copy should be sent to your agent automatically. However, Revenue

Inland Revenue   Reference 272 029955

Income Tax

Income Tax (Schedule A or Schedule D) and
Class 4 National Insurance Contributions   Date of issue
                                                 27 NOV 1993
YEAR ENDING 5 APRIL 1994

07728   272   Issued by

MR B FRANKLIN   R A STONE
POSTCODE MANSIONS   HM INSPECTOR OF TAXES
CHEOPS TOWN   TRIASSIC 3
                                 QUATERNARY HOUSE

                                 Tel: 0734 64211

This notice is addressed to you personally as required by law. It
should be shown to your professional adviser or agent (if you have
one) IMMEDIATELY.
If you do not agree with the assessment you should appeal in
writing WITHIN 30 DAYS from the date of issue above.
If you also consider that the amount charged is excessive you may
apply to postpone some or all of the tax and/or Class 4 NIC (see
form 64D enclosed).
Interest is charged on late payment.

PAYABLE AT ACCOUNTS OFFICE CUMBERNAULD

RECONCILIATION   1993/94

AMOUNT PAYABLE	1st INST	2nd INST
TAX	1025.50	1025.50
NATIONAL ISURANCE	244.88	244.88
TOTAL	1270.38	1270.38
PAYABLE 1 JAN 1994	1270.38	
PAYABLE 1 JUL 1994		1270.38

Figure 8.1 *Assessment of tax (Please note that all names, addresses,
reference numbers and telephone numbers are fictitious.)*

MR B FRANKLIN   Assessment number
                                 272 DP 029955 9401

NOTICE OF ASSESSMENT 1993/94

Income and deductions (E = estimated)   £
                                                          14474

CANDLE MAKER

TRADING DEDUCTIONS
Capital Allowances   360

                                                            360
                          TOTAL CHARGEABLE   14114
_____

Allowances
Class 4 Nic Relief   245
Personal Allowance   3445
Married Allowance   1720

TOTAL   5410   5410

Amount chargeable to tax   8704

Lower rate @ 20% on   £2500   500.00
Basic rate @ 25% on   £6204   1551.00

Net tax payable   2051.00

CLASS 4 NATIONAL INSURANCE PAYABLE
Profit   14114
Lower Limit   6340
Charged at 6.30% on   7774
AMOUNT PAYABLE   489.76

NOTES

Figure 8.1   *continued*

errors sometimes occur, and if your agent's name is not shown, you need to contact your agent with details of the assessment at once.

- *Timescale*

  The paragraph sets out the timescale for action – you have 30 days to appeal against the assessment, or postpone tax shown as due if you disagree with the figures. Second, there may be information specific to you, eg a reminder that you have to submit an outstanding tax return or other details.

- *Notice to pay*

  This is a table of figures showing the tax and National Insurance that are being demanded, with the total amounts and the dates that payment is due. What is the date shown for payment of tax? Usually it will be 1 January or 1 July. Otherwise it is 30 days from the date of issue. This gives you an idea of the urgency of the position. If you think the figures are not correct, you will want to pay only the correct amount of tax on the due date. If this is close at hand, you will need to consider making a postponement application. The procedure is considered below.

Right-hand side

- *Assessment number*

  This is the number you need to quote if you disagree with the figures.

- *Income and deductions*

  - This is followed by a description of the source of income, eg electrician, property developer, architect. Check that it is correct.

  - Against this description there will be a figure, which represents your gross taxable income. If you have sent accounts in to the Revenue for this year, and they have been accepted, check the figures with your accounts. The intricate part of operations here is to relate the accounting year to the tax year, although the system is due to change and in 1996 a simpler system should apply.

  - You can identify the set of accounts to use like this:

    1. Identify the year of assessment – the 'tax year' on the left-hand side of the assessment. This could be, for

example, the year ending 5 April 1994.

This represents a tax year starting on 6 April 1993 and ending on 5 April 1994. It could also be shown as 1993–94; this year would run from 6 April 1993 to 5 April 1994.

2. Go back one tax year. If your assessment is for the year to 5 April 1994, go back to the year to 5 April 1993. This represents the period from 6 April 1992 to 5 April 1993.

3. You now want the set of accounts which ended in this tax year. For example, if you prepare accounts to December each year, the correct accounts would be those to December 1992.

–   Now that you have the accounts, check that the profit shown on the assessment, and the capital allowances given, agree with the accounts. If they do not, you should make an appeal.

–   Check the arithmetic on the assessment!

–   If you have either just started in business or are ceasing self-employment, the position is more complex and you may well need professional advice.

–   Are the figures estimated? If the figure shown as gross taxable income is prefaced by an 'E' it is estimated. Estimated figures are usually round numbers. Estimated assessments are raised for a variety of reasons: sometimes an estimated assessment is raised even when the correct figures are with the Revenue. You can make a formal appeal against an estimated assessment, using the steps outlined below (pages 120–21).

*   *Trading deductions*

Under this heading there will usually be an entry for capital allowances. The figure against this description is deducted from your gross income. This gives you the figure described either as 'net assessment' or the 'total chargeable'.

*   *Allowances*

Under this heading there may be a number of allowances shown: your personal allowance, married couple's allowance, any relief due for pension payments, loan interest and Class 4

National Insurance. The total of these allowances is then shown.

- Check that no allowances are missing. You can do this by comparing the list with the claims you made on your income tax return.
- If you have more than one source of income, the question of how your allowances are split between your different sources of income may arise. It may be that allowances are set against another source of income. In this case, there may be a deduction from the total allowances shown on the assessment. If so, at the bottom of the page, there will be a heading 'Allocation of allowances: given elsewhere'. This will explain where the allowances have been given.

- *Calculation of tax*
  The total figure for allowances is deducted from the figure shown as 'total chargeable' or 'net assessment', and this produces the 'amount chargeable to tax'. The tax is calculated and the result is shown as 'net tax payable'.

- *Class 4 National Insurance payable*
  Under this heading the Class 4 calculation will be shown.

Other types of assessment

There are a number of other types of assessment. These range from partnership assessments to capital gains tax assessments to assessments of income from employment and investment income. The most common are probably partnership and investment income assessments.

- *Partnership assessments*
  Assessments for individual partners in a business are similar to the assessments for sole traders explained above. The main difference is that there is an additional assessment issued in the name of the partnership itself. This shows a division of profit between the partners and the total tax payable. The assessments addressed to the individual partners show how this tax bill has been made up. The steps for checking partnership assessments are as outlined above.

- *Investment income assessments*
  These are usually simpler than self-employed assessments. There is no Class 4 National Insurance, for example, and the

tax is usually due in one sum on 1 January. The complication lies in the fact that you are often being taxed on the gross income of last year, not that of the current year. There may be adjustments made through your tax coding in consequence, particularly if you are in receipt of a pension.

How to disagree

The last page of the booklet that arrives with your tax assessment is an appeal form. You can use this form – or simply write to the tax office – if you disagree with the figures.

To raise an objection, you must write to the Revenue within 30 days of the assessment being issued, stating the grounds for your challenge. This procedure is called lodging an appeal. Strictly speaking, an appeal is made against the income figure.

If you also want to alter the amount of tax being demanded, you must make a postponement application. This does not have to be done within 30 days, as long as you have at least raised a written objection to the figures within this period. In practice it is usually convenient to do both at the same time.

If you apply to postpone payment of tax, you should state your grounds for doing so. These may be the same as those for the appeal. Additional grounds would include:

- Personal allowance or married couple's allowance shown is incorrect or too low.
- No relief given for pension contributions paid.
- You are due additional relief for loan interest paid.

If you decide to postpone tax, remember that interest will run against you if you under-pay tax. Interest starts to run from the date that the tax is shown as being due. If you over-pay tax, a different timescale applies before you will receive interest from the Revenue. Usually you will have to wait at least 12 months before interest begins to accrue.

Once you have made your appeal and postponement, you should receive agreement from the Revenue within 28 days. In due course, you should receive a revised assessment which you can check all over again. If you and the Revenue are in accord, you should now have figures that you can accept. If not... go back to stage one!